T0063153

You Are *Already There*

an experience in consciousness

Robert Gregory

BALBOA
PRESS
A DIVISION OF HAY HOUSE

Balboa Press books may be ordered through booksellers or by contacting:

Balboa Press
A Division of Hay House
1663 Liberty Drive
Bloomington, IN 47403
www.balboapress.com.au
1-(877) 407-4847

ISBN: 978-1-4525-0927-3 (sc)
ISBN: 978-1-4525-0930-3 (e)

Printed in the United States of America

Balboa Press rev. date:03/14/2013

Introduction

This book I have put together are my own thoughts on what I could make out of what I experienced; the experience of dissolving into nothingness. I have now put a label to it, the label is called *Awakening*, or *Enlightenment*. These words are not what I experienced but are the nearest descriptions I could find to tell my story. Of course these labels have been used by many who also have had their own experience of what they labelled as Awakening, Enlightenment or whatever.

If you yourself experience this dissolving into nothingness after this so called Enlightenment, then you may use the same labels, or even make one up. It really doesn't matter. The experience is never the label, even the experience isn't what was experienced, but you will have to find out for yourself. So happy reading and may you lose or find what you need to, but remember not to take anything that I have said serious, and also don't believe in anything that you read here. Find out what I have said for yourself, prove it for yourself, after all it's your life.

Robert Gregory

When life seems to do nothing but pass you by
Take a step back and look life in the eye
ee things clearly by rising above
Taking the stance of trust and love,

Have faith and patience, kindness and care
Hopes and dreams may float in the air,
But respect and honour thyself be true
And await your fate as chosen by you.

Jules,
Super Moderator from www.spiritualforums.com

Contents

Poems by Palden

It Begins . . .

Tony Parsons was one of the first authors I read after my apparent Awakening. Before this I had no idea what happened to me, but when I read that Tony walked through the park and was no longer there, I thought "WoW, that's me!" That's what happened, and of course now I had a label to stick onto it.

I then read as many books as I could on others who have had this same experience, some make it all sound so mystical and there are others who make it all sound so easy, I prefer the latter because in my case it was easy, but why shouldn't it? After all its who or what we are. It's funny, here we are all these little creatures called humans on this piece of star dust asking these deep, deep, questions, it makes me think of the little fleas on a dog asking the same questions. One comes up and says, can't you see, it's God, not the dog, can you feel it, we are part of Him, we go where He goes.

I don't consider myself as Enlightened, when I say that, I'm really playing with you. You see the ego mind will grab this and run with it, WoW, I'm Enlightened, unfortunately men like Jesus didn't play the game as I would and in Jesus' case He got crucified for coming straight out and saying "I am the truth, I am the way . . ." for me I don't think I like the idea of being crucified.

In truth we as the mind body can never be Enlightened, the body is just a construction of blood bone and all the rest. The mind thinks its this body and when the mind thinks its Enlightened it doesn't go beyond the mind, it just stays stagnant and rotting away with the body. Enlightenment is beyond the mind body, this is where it comes to a dead end in trying to describe the indescribable, we can only use pointers, even the pointers after a time will become useless and need to be dropped. One can only enter Heaven alone, everything else will fall away as you get closer and closer, and BANG!!, you will go off like gunpowder, whereas before you were only like green wood, the fire of truth could never ignite you no matter how hard you tried.

The reality is that no matter how hard you try, you can never reach Enlightenment, you will only get in the way. When you are not in the way, when you are not you, or the you you thought was you, Enlightenment will be there, it was always there, the problem was you were always in the way. Stop believing you can be Enlightened and just give in, surrender, let Consciousness take you out of the prison that you, your ego has put you in.

Just relax, go into your inner *SELF* and just be, feel the silence, when the mind raises its nasty little head with its raving and ranting, just relax, be in the back seat watching the mind. You will soon see that the mind isn't even you, you will even start to think, gee is that me, you may as in my case start to have a big belly laugh, this is cool, the ego mind has now been caught out, the jig is up.

As a child I was so inquisitive, I loved to be out in nature catching butterflies and bees, everything around me was so exciting. I remember as a second grader I would take my little Imaginary friends, or I think they were imaginary, to school and they would live under my deck, and when it was time to go home, I would put them back in my school bag and take them home. At home they would all follow me around, in the bathroom we would all play together. As I grew up like most children I let go of my friends as I was taught by everyone around me, that such things were childish, so I went along with the game of life, for the better? I don't think so.

Shot and Paranoid

When I left school, I then attached another label on myself, called a baker, I worked in the bakery for about 14 years, I had to leave because of a gunshot injury. Wow!, a gunshot injury!? Well of course you want to hear about that. It all started when I was about 22 years old, my friends and I went for a swim at a swimming hole just out of town, we had been driving around all night, as you do when young and inquisitive. We then decided to go for a swim. It was about 2 am in the morning when we reached the swimming hole, we all ran down to the water and discovered that it was too damn cool to enter, so we retreated back to the car, I was the driver.

On the way back from the swimming hole I remembered that I was thinking, gee, I can't wait to drop my mates off, as I was so tired and couldn't wait to get home for bed, what I didn't know in those seconds, was going to be a life changing event, that would change my life forever. BANG!!, There I was driving and now I was in a reel of film, in a terrifying movie played before me, it felt within those seconds that it wasn't me in the movie, running through my mind.

My ankle felt numb and I remember that I went to feel it and my fingers went into a gaping hole. I went into instant shock, my friend who was asleep next to me awoke, and also panicking, took the steering wheel from me, but lost control of the car which screamed off the road spinning round and round. I could see my life as they say flashing before me, it was so weird, it was just like I always heard, of others talking about their life flashing before them.

When the car came to a stop all hell broke out, there were three friends of mine running around panicking, I was laying back with my leg raised, all I could think of, was that this nightmare was going to come closer to me, to finish me off.

I also remember that one of my friends yelled out to me, not to move my leg, he said it looks like the ankle might come off—well this really had me going, I have never felt so much panic. My friends started to move out to the side of the road to hail someone down, but no one would stop, and out of the blue a cab pulled over. Now this was my angel in a beautiful black and white taxi, he radioed into base, and not long after the police and ambulance arrived, and the next thing I remember is waking up in hospital.

My ankle was saved but I have no movement with it, and I am on a disability pension today because of it.

This terror pushed me away from humanity and more into myself, I was now paranoid.

I was always spiritual without knowing that I was, or knowing anything about the label of spirituality. The first time I saw the Hare Krishna's singing and dancing in the city, I was stunned, something within me just clicked, I just had to find out more about these strange people. I knew that within me they would show me something that would change my life forever.

So off I went reading all their books, not really at that time understanding them spiritually, but there was an understanding deep within, the feeling of, yea, now I know, yes, I get it—its really hard to explain.

I was about 15 years old at this time, I was starting to feel like I didn't belong here in this world, humans were like other creatures to me but I never told anyone, being 15 and all, a 15 year old had to be a 15 year old of course.

Because I felt I didn't belong here, I started to feel a little scared that one of these creatures called humans might hurt me, I was very shy and as my mother always said, highly strung.

Through most of my life I did attract those who wanted to hurt me, I was sexually abused by an older man when I was about 13 years old, this seemed to continue throughout my younger life. I once had a man who held a knife to me and made me do all sorts of things, I was so scared. I later shared a unit with a friend who sold drugs, here my life was threatened twice, again I had a knife to me asking me where the drugs were.

After I was shot I withdrew from the world, after so many years I started to develop what I know now as schizophrenia. I was paranoid with people I didn't know, and started to hear voices—I couldn't even go into a coffee shop. When I tried to I could hear all these voices laughing at me, saying things like "Look at him who does he think he is coming into here?" I also had voices arguing in my head, one would be cursing me and the other would be defending me, I was in between these voices, it was hell.

This continued on for a few years until one day I just lost it, I was doing a job for an elderly couple from church, I was doing gardening and was pushing a wheel barrow with clippings, when all of a sudden I could see the elderly couple all dismembered lying in the wheel barrow, it freaked me right out.

I have always been interested in the Christian faith, and was a member of the Seventh Day Adventist Church, I was about 17. I felt that I wasn't getting what I thought I needed, so I started to go back to my Hare Krishna books that I read when I was younger.

These were a great help but still I wanted more, I soon became disheartened with life and all that I have gathered from its smorgasbord of belief systems.

I started to feel like I didn't want to be in this strange world any more, I started to feel detached from the body, I would look into the mirror and what I saw wasn't me, it was a stranger, my mind body was in automatic and I had no part of it, I was like a robot.

Life was a numbness, it felt like I wasn't in the body any more and it was getting hard to function. I was now on anti-psychotics and this didn't help either, I just slept all the time, while I was sleeping I didn't have to feel the mind body that was drowning me in all of

its programming, that had been collected over the years of my so called life.

I was too scared to commit suicide and felt like I was a coward, I would sit with a knife digging it into myself, just wishing I could push it right through me.

I began to fear the news on the television thinking that all those bad people would come over to Australia and get me. I would listen to the TV, thinking that everything I thought was also said by the news reader, I was really paranoid, fearing my own shadow.

I began to hate religion and everything to do with it, after all it told me that I was a low life sinner, every time I went to church, all they told me is that I was a sinner and I needed Jesus, I thought fuck Jesus!

The Disappearance

One night when I was just laying down to go to sleep I started
to drift away into what seemed to be a void, I just let myself
go with it, I drifted more and more into nothingness, whatever
that was.

All of a sudden I was gone. There was no me, there was only pure
space, I felt like I could see all the stars and planets, the whole
Cosmos was opening, I say that I felt these things, but the truth is
as I said, I wasn't there.

There was a sense from within that this I, was everything that there
IS, in those seconds or minutes I can't recall, I could feel every single
soul as One, it was beautiful.

When I came back to the body—or was I always there?—I was
changed forever.

I remember I started to laugh, I didn't really know why but it felt
like I just found something, that I was searching for the whole of my
life, I wasn't really searching for anything spiritual, well consciously
that is, and this thing that I found had no name, nothing, it was just a
feeling of great relief that every cell throughout my body knew of.

Now I was walking for the first time above the earths surface, I
now knew what Jesus meant by walking on the water, the crap of
the world was far below my feet, it could no longer touch me or
harm me.

The idea of me being a Jesus or God, that I thought of at times was
now gone, I now knew within that that this way of thinking was

dualistic and to say that I was Jesus or God was only separating me from what IS.

Robert was no longer there, his story was still played along, but now in automatic mode, the higher Consciousness now was all there was, every now and then, I AM would play the game of pretending it was Robert, this was real fun, he's so cheeky and sometimes can be a pain in the butt, for those who are still asleep, in thinking they are in full control of who they think they are.

Robert now liked to burst bubbles and dreams, to give someone something they believe they need is to only put them into a deeper sleep.

I felt like the prince who kissed the sleeping beauty, to Awaken her but what I didn't know was that the sleeping beauty didn't want to be awakened.

Beyond Labels

I have a friend who owns a New Age shop, he sells mainly books plus the things you would expect to find in a new age shop. I have been frequenting William's shop for many years not really knowing what to read or not to read, but after the experience I apparently had, William out of the blue came up to me and started to recommend me books to read. In all the years I have been in his shop he has never showed an interest in me, at least not that I know of.

The books he showed me were about non-dualism, I thought "what on earth is this all about?" But I was in for a surprise.

The first book I read I have to admit I don't remember the authors name, I never really took any notice of the authors of any books that I read, but I remember the book described what seem to be the experience I had on that crazy night, I was hooked, these books were made for me!

What I was doing now without realising, was putting labels on the experience I apparently had, making them now second hand.

It doesn't matter how many other stories we hear from others, and their so called Awakening, it is never what IS, what IS can only be Realised when there is no one there, no books or authors, not even me as Robert. Its an individual experience, and when I say individual I don't mean the individual self as the ego, but the individual Consciousness.

I wouldn't have a clue what the concept of what Consciousness is intellectually, all I know is that there was a disappearance into nothingness and in this nothingness all was revealed, but ask me what that was and I cannot tell you.

All I can do is try to describe what was and point you to what was, there you will have to cross the river all by yourself, and even yourself cannot enter this crossing.

What I do agree with what others have said in my readings, is that you have to drop everything you were ever taught, who you are, every ideology, every belief system that you have clung to, must be discarded and only then if you are under grace, will you disappear into the void.

In fact you cannot do anything to get there, for who is trying to get there? Ask yourself that question, who is trying to get there?

When you ask yourself this question, go deeper and deeper until you find the one who wants Enlightenment, the one who has been searching for this freedom.

You will find that there is no one there, its just the ego playing its game of wanting, wanting, wanting.

It's when the wanting, the clinging, the needing is dropped, that the Source of Consciousness will pour in, when you get out of the way Consciousness will finally enter. You have been so full of yourself that Consciousness never could enter, but in all Truth Consciousness was always there, paradox after paradox you will find when listening to the Truth, or the signs that point to the truth.

This is the reason why it is so hard to talk about, myself I was never a good public speaker or writer, so for me its even harder to even point others to this so called Truth.

Love and its Source

C onsciously I was never really after anything in my life, but I felt there may have been an inner urge pulling me towards its SELF, I also feel that we all have this within ourselves.

Many feel the urge to gamble, drink alcohol, find as much sex as they can but all these are the distortion of what is really trying to get our attention. We even have multitudes of people worshipping sports, it's like a religion to them, they even worship the players as if they're gods.

This pulling is what I call Love, its like the rivers that are trying to get back to the ocean where they originally came from. The same is with us, we are Consciousness, and the Consciousness that we are within the mind body, is in Love with its SELF, this love pulls it Self back to its pure Source.

When we are in love with another we are in most cases unaware of this magnetism, in most cases we distort this pure attraction with neurotic behaviour, we start to cling to the other because we feel we are not whole without them, when all the time we can never be anything but wholeness, it's just that subconsciously we know that we are part of the other also, but we are also part of everyone else.

To realise this we now know that we are in LOVE with all, we are ONE with all, this is the real meaning of love thy neighbour as thy SELF.

We as humans seem to cling to our own selected few, such as family members, spouses, children and even our pets; we attach what we believe is love to these, but this isn't what love is, love isn't only for the selected few.

Love is our pure Source, its what we are. Human love seems to run ok as long as the other stands up to our expectations, its there one day, and gone the next.

Myself, I don't like the word love, it actually brings a bad taste to my mouth, it seems as if there is so much of it about, its talked about and written about, but when one looks with an inner heart, there is nothing of true Love anywhere, the selected few keep silent about it, not flaunting it like some prize medal that has been won by catching ones self a prize wife or husband.

I have been through this playground of throwing love back and forth like a football, I have been addicted to another human being believing I was nothing without that person, all this time I thought this was love.

I remember thinking once, gee, I didn't realise love was so hard and so cruel, but there I was again jumping into it like a addicted drug addict, jumping into his next fix.

When there is this realisation from within, there is no more wanting someone or something to make you complete, you now realise that you have always been complete. You are completed in every single living and none living thing.

When we believe we are separate we then feel as if we need something to cling to, if not a security blanket, another human under the blanket. True love isn't security, true love doesn't protect you, it allows you to do whatever you want, it even lets you die.

Religion

eligion, well, where do I begin? I was baptised as a Seventh
Day Adventist back in 1974, I was only 17 then and didn't
quite know what the hell I was doing. My parents were never
into religion and I—out of 4 children—was the first and only to be
baptised. I didn't stay long in the church and left to run wild in the
sinful world of drinking and fornicating, well that's what the church
lead me to believe.

I returned back to the same church 23 years later, this inner tugging
was starting to get stronger within me. Like I said, consciously I
didn't really want anything but there was this inner intuition, a deep
feeling that I was going to discover something of greatness.

I now started to study my bible seriously, I would attend bible
study once a week and sometimes twice, I was really soaking it
all up.

At first I never questioned what I was being told, I was being
hypnotised by dogma without realising it.

I felt guilt and even threw out all my porn, which I regretted later,
now was ripe for my calm underlining psychosis to erupt into a
volcano of spewing anger.

I started to hate myself, I heard voices calling me every name
under the sun, I felt filthy inside, the sermons at church felt like
they were directed right at me, calling me a sinner over and over, the
church never really told us things like, how special we are to God.
It always put God and and his Son Jesus, on a high pedestal that we

could never reach, all I wanted at that time was to reach this God and punch him right in the fucking mouth and kick his Son right up the ass.

Yes, Christianity started to lose its flavour in my life and I began to go to church a lot less often.

This is when I also began to ask the deep questions about life, questions like why the hell am I here, what the hell is it all about, it all just made no sense to me, I was losing it, I was drowning in my own insanity.

I have to also add, that this guilt that I was experiencing, was also stoked by my mothers death, a death that hunted me for years.

Guilt

My father died when he was only 48 years old, he was a heavy smoker all his life and later started to have heart problems, he was admitted to hospital where they did test on him but unfortunately he developed a blood clot in his leg.

The doctor on the early shift was suppose to let the later doctor know, to administer a drip to dissolve the clot, this never happened and my dad died that night of a blocked valve from the blood clot.

My mum only four years later was diagnosed with colon cancer, she had radiation treatment that seem to work, but this was only wishful thinking, three years later they found another growth on the side of her neck.

I remember the day she came home and told me, she asked me to help her make up her mind, to have or not to have chemotherapy. I told her that I think she shouldn't have it, did I make the wrong decision?

I have always been interested in the human body and always wanted to be a doctor. Well to be a doctor means a lot of hard study from school through to university, of about 6 years of ass-up face-down study, nah, I soon gave that idea up, just too lazy I suppose?

I always loved\to read books on the anatomy and physiology of the human body, secretly dreaming that I was a medical student. One day I read an add in the paper, on becoming a Naturopath, I thought yea this will compensate for my wish to be a doctor—subconsciously of course—and off I went to become a naturopath after a subsequent 5 years of study.

I studied remedial massage, herbal medicine, iridology and everything else that one needs to learn to hang their sign up, and in my case, pretend to be a doctor sign.

I never really got fully into being a naturopath as I found out I was too damn scared and didn't have enough confidence, but I did have my few patients that were always happy to come to me for a good massage, and a iris diagnoses but all this came to a halt. Damn too lazy again.

Well like all mothers my mum was proud of me being a naturopath, and I often gave her a massage to prove my wonderful abilities.

So when my mum came home that afternoon and told me that the doctors have found another cancer, and it was a real bad one at that, I felt I just had to do something, after all I was the big naturopath in her life. So when my mum asked me if I thought she should have Chemo or not, well what more could I say, especially when most naturopaths don't really like their patients on such things as this poison called Chemo, I just had to say no.

Mum went to a naturopath that I knew, and he gave her a cleansing diet that was design to help remove toxins from her body, she then started to eat a semi vegetarian diet.

She was going well and everything looked great, she felt like she had more energy than she had for a long while, she also wasn't experiencing any pain, but of course things can change and they did.

Mum started to feel a lump coming through her left shoulder right between her collar bone and shoulder bone, she also was starting to lose a lot of weight.

From then on things started to look not that good, but we held onto hope and I think between both of us we pretended that it would all work out, but cancer just doesn't seem to obey our wishes; it has a mind of its own and that mind was angry.

Mum was now nearly a skeleton and it was cruel to see her like this, but we kept believing that everything would be ok, at least it made us feel better.

Well like all things, they soon or later come to an end and mum was admitted to hospital where her and my dreams were shattered.

The nurse came to the door, "Mrs. Gregory would you like some pudding?" Mum looked at me as if to wait for my approval, as I did keep an eye on what she ate, I looked at her and said "Of course mum." I think it was the best damn pudding she ever had, it was also the last damn pudding she would ever have.

After my mother passed away I was so devastated and full of guilt. I remember at the funeral service I felt and could hear voices saying, "Look at that murderer, he killed his mother", this rang through my mind over and over.

Guilt really eats at you, my brother who died in a car accident caused my mum and dad great guilt, they blamed each other for buying him the car that he got killed in. He was 16 at the time and because he was too young to drive his mate used to drive for him.

It was an October afternoon when I heard the knock at the door, dad came running through to mum and there was screaming and chaos; my brother was dead.

Dad died young, only 48, and as you already know mum died not long after, I believe that guilt was behind most of what lead them to die so young.

Guilt really had a hold on me, it was sending me mad, I just hated myself so much and just wanted to die. The voices were now becoming worse than ever, telling me how much of a bad ass I was, they would keep telling me that I was a murderer, that should not be here.

I knew that I needed help and I went to see my GP who referred me to a psychiatrist. I was put onto anti-psychotics straight away, these made me so tired that I could hardly drive my car, I was so numb and the medication made it worse. All I wanted was to sleep, beautiful sleep.

While I was sleeping I wasn't here to feel the guilt and emotional pain, I just wished I would never wake up again, I now know that this was the mind body trying to keep me away from what was to come very soon, what was to take away this pain.

Being disappointed with the church also was a heavy burden, this God and His son just didn't make any sense to me, at least not at this moment in time.

It now came to a time when I was in the process of dropping everything I was told or learnt, about religion or spirituality, heaven sounded like a place for guilt ridden sinners and I didn't want anything to do with it.

So the time was ripe for the biggest show of my life, an act that didn't include me, but at the same time included everything that there IS.

After what I found out to be what was called an Enlightened experience, my whole life as Robert changed.

The guilt started to leave me and I was at a wonderful peace with all that there is, I would go out at night and look up at the stars and I would feel them, I was part of them, it was truly my home, the Cosmos. What a Mansion God has given me, maybe there's a Mansion, a Cosmos for all of those who become Awakened? "In my fathers house there are many Mansions."

I now felt my own Religion growing within, my own connection to God, my own Being, Consciousness, I have now taken my rightful position, setting at the right hand of GOD.

God now was making sense to me, I could read the bible and really see for the first time the hidden meaning that was staring right at me all along.

I Can See Clearly Now

It's funny when one becomes so called Awakened, you suddenly start to see everything come alive all around you, the colours are brighter, the sky more blue, its like falling in love for the very first time, not like the outer shell of love that seems to be more of an addiction to be clung to.

All of a sudden you notice books that explain or try to explain this new magic. As I have already said, in the shop that I have been frequenting for a number of years, for the first time the owner took an interest in me, telling me that he knew what books I should read, he directed me to the non-dualism section. I ended up reading just about every one of those books, it felt as if I finally found kindred spirits who thought and had the same experience as I did.

The one author that always comes to mind is Eckhart Tolle, he explains this new love found experience so well and so simple, in fact when the Realisation hits you, you just can't believe how simple it is, and it was there within all along; the Cosmic joke as they say.

The problem with Religion is that it keeps you away from the truth, it teaches you that truth is something to be obtained, something that you have to find outside of yourself.

Most of Christianity teaches you like a child and never lets you grow in the Christ that you truly are, it teaches you that Jesus was the only Christ and you can only be saved by His blood, and by His death.

The trap of most Religion, is to tell you that you are a sinner and you need to be forgiven every time you sin, it makes you feel as if you need the church, but this is only using a belief as a crutch, just to feel safe, just in case what they tell you is true.

I see this as childish, just like children who lie, steal, cheat, call others names, and hit other children, it teaches you that you are a very naughty boy or girl, and need to get down on your knees and beg big Daddy for forgiveness.

Sin is really immaturity and ignorance of your true Reality, when you Realise that you are ONE with everyone else, you simply don't want to steal or hurt another, to do so is to hurt yourself, this is to truly know what the truth of sin means.

The new testament sin means, to be 'off target' but if your target is your true SELF or God, how could you ever miss, it is just too big.

As Jesus supposedly said in the bible, "Father forgive them for they no not what they do", if they knew that Jesus was their very own Self or represented their true SELF, they wouldn't have crucified him, but they were in ignorance of this and this is what sin is; ignorance.

We are all like Royal descendents of heaven, of the same family, of the same Consciousness. The great joke is that we have forgotten this, and continually told that we are just a mind body organism, just a sheep to be led around by some imaginary God in the sky, or if not a religious God, or a God of the state, country, tradition, or even sports.

You are much more than this, you are everything that there IS. Feel it, go outside and look up at the stars, all that what you see is you, wow, isn't that much better than a crazy God that just can't wait to have his way with you?

EGO Bashing

At the time I started to devour books on non-dualism, I came across a book called, *A Course In Miracles*, also referred to as *ACIM*. When one looks at the book they find no author on the cover, however in the preface of the course one finds the name Helen Schucman, who describes in her own words the process by which the material came to fruition. Schucman claimed to have written the material, with the help of William Thetford, based on the dictation of an inner Voice, which voice Schucman identified as Jesus.

Now I don't know if this is true or not but what the book has to say is extremely beautiful, it makes the bible look as a shadow compared to this beautiful book of deep wisdom.

I could see in the channelled writings of this book a deep truth that I intuitively had always understood, it was like, yes, its all coming back, I remember NOW.

Its strange how words when spoken in truth ignite something deep within, not an intellectual knowing, but a deeper Knowing that has always been Known.

This is what makes it so hard to convey to others that haven't entered the silence within, and of course in all truth there is no one to know this truth, how could the mind body ever understand such things?

The mind body is only a programmed organism, we are conditioned right from birth until the day we die. We believe we are separate and in full control, if this is the case why are so many not happy, and why have we always fought and killed each other.

As the mind body we have no choice but to follow our program, the ego hates to hear this and will rebel against anyone who declares this, if you find that you feel resentment towards these words, then maybe you should take a look at your ego, if it will ever let you.

The paradox is you have to drop the ego but at the same time there is no ego to drop, the ego is only an illusion, how can you drop an illusion? Well you Realise that it is an illusion and like all illusions, once it is Realised you don't take much notice of it any more, as they say, the snake has been seen for what it was, only a piece of rope. You are no longer frightened of the rope that you mistook all along as a snake. The rope is still there but the illusion of it being a snake is gone.

The ego now is seen for what it is, just programming, but now you are no longer under the hypnotic trance, of the programming being you, that is your true SELF.

Your true SELF is Consciousness, You made you, Consciousness is your life force, it's everything. There is nothing outside of Consciousness, Consciousness is just weaving its SELF like a giant tapestry. You and I are part of that thread within the tapestry, and just like a beautiful tapestry mat every piece of material is beautiful in its own way, the stars, the planets, the trees, everything, and everything is ONE, this Oneness is what true Love is, it binds us all together, it holds us in its bosom. This is the first step in Realising your true nature, to realise that you are not the mind body, the next step is to realise that there is no one to realise, when one gets to this state of no state, one is no longer there, this is the disappearance I spoke of earlier, in what I or the *apparent* I disappeared into.

The course of miracles talks of Idols as an image that we use to replace our true SELF, we can even see ourselves in another, and unknowingly try to cling to the other projecting ourselves on to them. We are like a parasite living a life that we believe is also us, all the time stunting the others spiritual growth.

As one knows, many parents also do this to their children—living their life through them—a life that they could never manage on their own.

The ego is the biggest idol of all. Many believe that the idol is something outside of ourselves, such as a statue, building, something tangible but this isn't really so. The ego who we believe is our self, keeps us always trying to satisfy this self, this then brings us frustration and misery, for the ego can never be satisfied, as soon as you are a millionaire it wants another million.

When we Awaken to this parasite, we then realise that all of our life was controlled by it, but we also have to be on guard that we don't replace this ego with its brother, the ego basher. Many then try to control this parasite, they try to hammer it into submission, not realising they are creating another, that now becomes the internal police officer.

This internal police officer now tries to make the rules of the game—and that is all it will be, just another game, another story—it will believe itself to be free, it will believe itself to be above the world and all the other ego's.

There are so many of these ego's calling themselves Gurus and the like, they try to teach others how to bash their ego's into submission, and all the time not realising themselves that *there is no ego to bash into submission*. Who's going to do the bashing? The mind body? The ego? There is nothing to get rid of; nothing to bash into submission.

Ask yourself where is this ego? Try to pinpoint it then deal with it, of course you'll never find it, so then how is one to be free from this illusionary ego?

Well forget about the ego, it's not there. Go within and discover for yourself the silence within you, of course while you are doing this, the illusional ego will try to get back your attention and in most cases in a big and more powerful way. It will feel as if it's kicking and screaming, but just like a child trying to get its own way, ignore it, remember it's only an illusion and you have had a lifetime to condition yourself to believe in it, so it won't leave overnight.

In a way we now are dehypnotising the mind, we are now realising that we are not the ego, that we are pure Essence, pure Consciousness or if you like pure LOVE. This new found LOVE is who you are, its not the surface or outer love that is thrown around like a football, this surface love is what most are addicted to, believing it is true unadulterated LOVE but again, it's only the illusion.

There is so much written about this love, but at the same time there is so much we don't know about this love. We can never know about love, we can only be what love is, we can only be who we truly are, but whatever label you attach to it is not what IS. I think we need to drop all these silly childish words, that we have come to believe to be what they are not, of course when we realise this we then can still use these labels, but now we are using them only as pointers, not the real deal.

The Real Deal

The real deal is far beyond this shadow that we see all around us, the killing in the name of love for our country, in the name of our psychotic gods. We seem to dish out this love to those who we believe deserve it more than the other. This love is only what I could call neurotic love, not even love at all, just a neuroses that we believe to be a wonderful thing to be achieved by the selected few.

The reality is there is no such thing as love, as there is no such thing as the ego, both formulated by the mind body programming, programmes that we have been feed by our parents, television and fairy-tale books, that describe how the beautiful princess and prince lived happy ever after—this is what most of us believe to be love.

So if I had to put a name or label to this love that is pointed to, I would say that this love is our own True-Being. Just like the blood that runs through our bodies, this love animates through all that there is. This life force is our true Being, or our true so called SELF, it never goes anywhere, it cannot die or be born, its closer to us than anything outside of us could ever be.

To truly fall in love is to fall into your SELF, those who are not ready will only drown and thrash about, this I believe is what happens in the case of such mental disorders as schizophrenia. One is so in tuned to the inner and outer life that they cannot cope with the power of this over stimulated inner Consciousness, just as calm water when boiled bubbles and with lots of movement, when the water cools again it is calm, this is what the inner unconscious realisation is. If one is under grace then one will Awaken, but only if one is under the grace of what could be many past lives, that have brought one to this grace and the Awakening of ones true SELF.

This true Self that I am trying to talk about really isn't anything new—it has always been—there was no time when it wasn't, like the Tao that cannot be named. Whatever I try to say about it is never going to be it. When there has been this apparent Awakening by no one, all one can really do is to point the other to their own SELF; this is the only SELF that I know of.

We don't all have a separate self that we all need to enter, there is only ONE SELF, *my* true SELF is also *your* true SELF, even by saying true SELF is not quite right, this then sounds like there must be another SELF, so you can see why we need to be careful when trying to point the other.

But once the SELF has been realised then there is no more you can know about it, anything that you add is only going to take you away from what IS.

I am no poet and to describe this apparent disappearance using the mind body can be quite hard, but then one can be a great poet and write beautiful poetry on love, melting the heart of their reader, but this has no guarantee that he or she knows what true love is. This is no excuse on my behalf, but I must let the reader know for the hope to have them read on and make their own minds up, if this is for them or not, some believe they need something complicated, something to get their teeth into, but this is only because of the ego mind wanting to keep you away from this inner discovery, the discovery that will end the ego.

The end of the ego is to realise that the ego is nothing more than a collection of programmes or conditionings, that is seen to be who you are, now that you know this you now have something to meditate on, something to contemplate over in the silence of your inner Being.

Just like an alcoholic that realises that he is an alcoholic, he at least has taken the most important step of confessing the truth of his problem, if that is what it is to him. Now he is in the light and can see more clearly how his problem has affected his life, he can now take action.

Just as the addiction of something like alcohol takes time to let go, so is the same with the so called ego that one is so addicted to, the mind body has built up millions of receptors throughout the mind body that needs their fix each and every day.

This addiction can be anything from food to sex, even pain. The mind body can thrive on whatever keeps it alive, if you are one of those people who are always complaining about everything under the sun, be it the weather or whatever, you may be addicted to your own pain.

This pain doesn't necessarily have to be a wound to the body, it can be emotional pain, the pain of continually bringing up something bad from the past, even though it hurts you, you just can't seem to let it go, at least it gives you a story, so the ego will lead you to believe.

There is so much written about this that I don't really think its for me to calibrate over here, after all, I'm no psychiatrist, all I am interested in is showing you, or trying to point you to, how simple all this can be. I am just the average Joe Blow, I don't try to be some new-found Guru who just wants to set themselves up in business, we already have plenty of those.

I don't like attention and I don't want attention, maybe I am after attention in these words in front of you without even knowing consciously? It really doesn't matter when there has been this Awakening, the little tricks of the ego are seen for what they are, just like a magician pulling their tricks out in front of us, we know its only a trick but we are entertained by it and that's what it is like after this so called Awakening.

So now we know that its all hat tricks, now we can sit back and enjoy the ride—not taking it so serious. When one is Aware, we start to see the tricks performed by the others around us, and it can be very entertaining, your friends will wonder why you have that little smirk on your face.

Yes, a good sense of humour can be all you really need to disappear into your SELF, into your true Being. The best humour is when we can laugh at ourselves, in the Awakening you will Realise that the biggest joke of all was always you.

There are so many who just don't like to know that they are controlled by this magnificent person they believed themselves to be, they get insulted. These are the ones who really need to laugh at themselves, before they can even start to take baby steps towards their true Being. One reason for this is that when Consciousness is entered, you will see the joker you have always been, this can only be Realised by the humorist within.

It's Not Rocket Science

There is so much about this Awareness, this Enlightenment, it makes one think, what the hell is it, where do I begin???

Well, first of all you don't have to begin anywhere, you are already there, you can't be anywhere else but there, you see. It's easy, it's not rocket science, in fact the more knowledge you accumulate the more you must empty. Not that you must throw it all away, no, this knowledge can be useful but it will never get you to where you believe you want to be, when you have, or your apparent self has been to this place of no place, you then can return and use all the knowledge as your tools in life.

The inner Carpenter now has built his Mansion in Consciousness, and now can return and use the outer tools to make his life in this world more comfortable, it may be all an illusion like some will tell you, but at least it will NOW be a nice illusion, like a nice dream, much better than the nightmare that you have been living with.

There are a million and one ways that this Consciousness is described but to me I just see it as a giant pot of stew, an endless infinite stew, not in a giant pot but suspended in its own juices, juices that are also coagulated as its illusionary separate parts, its potatoes as planets, its carrots as you and I and all but ONE Stew, now doesn't that sound yummy?

The stew is within the carrots and the carrots are within the stew, we as the carrots are walking through this stew and its juices, but the juices are seen by the carrots as separate, the potatoes that we see out in the juices space we believe to be separate, but in fact the potatoes are also connected through its juices to the carrots.

To be the illusionary parts in this infinite Cosmos and to Realise that we are not separate from anything, or even part of anything, is to have an inner Awakening, this just can't be understood by the very illusionary mind, the mind will think it has understood this but its not really an inner Knowing at all, this is where it gets sticky, very sticky, this is where words start to fail and collapse.

I have never been into meditation, not in the general sense that is. I have however sat in contemplation, that is in observation, just looking and watching the mind trying to work it all out intellectually. When you finally notice the mind just giving in, go with that, surrender into that, just give up the whole idea of the mind ever understanding it.

In this surrender we start to feel calm because now the mind has been tamed from a roaring lion, it now feels like a kitten, it has given into the questioning of what it now knows to be impossible for it to ever have an answer.

So if there is anything we can do, then all one can do is to do nothing, and in that nothingness maybe, just maybe, Consciousness will recognize its SELF. But as I keep saying, it will never have anything to do with you, it will only happen when you are nowhere to be found, that sounds like a big let down doesn't it? But as long as you still think of it as a let down you're still there, in the mind.

When I say it will happen when you are not around, the truth is that its already there, it already has happened, there was never a time when it wasn't there. See this is why its so easy, you don't have to do anything as I keep saying.

The mind wants to make everything a challenge, it wants to climb Mt. Everest, it wants to go to the moon, the more difficult the more it feels as if it's a hero deserving a badge of honour.

I remember after the time I was shot, the ego not long after, began to think of the gun shot wound as a medal of great honour. It just loved to show its prized scar to anyone who would give it praise and tell it how awful it must have been, the pain body would even show itself in tears when describing the terror of that frightening night.

So you see the ego is so cunning, it's an expert of being the worlds best manipulator, the game is to always catch it out and shine the light of Consciousness on it.

You can make this into a game, you don't have to take it all so serious, like I keep saying its just an illusion so always remember that, just keep catching it out, pretty soon there will be no more to catch out, the game will be over.

Playing this game will always keep you awake and alert, it will keep you in the NOW, not in the past of remembrance, or in the future of false transference.

The ego will try to keep you in the past and the so called future, for it to be in the NOW is death to the ego, there's nothing for it to thrive on in the NOW, of course if you carry a story on from the NOW, the ego will take hold of it and own it for itself glorification.

What I am trying to describe is something that was known from within, as I have said Robert wasn't there, I am not trying to make a new belief system for others to follow, as I also have said there are plenty of these already, there's just an inner longing that just wants to compassionately attract all other rivers so that there's an emergence into the ocean of pure bliss, of pure Love, of Oneness. Even though this ocean of Consciousness is always there and has never changed, there's still the compassion to see all sentient beings happy in this beautiful Realisation of inner Consciousness.

When one is, or apparently has been reunited into their Being, there is nothing they can do after this but to invite all others, who are lost in the dream of illusion, it just becomes one's true nature to do so.

This love to see all as ONE, is so powerful, its not likened to the ego that will only want to make others see its own way, or belief, just for its own gratification. Like I have said there is no one there to be Awakened, there is no one there to feel self gratification, there is just what IS, there is just pure LOVE.

Get to know your false established ego, be the detective and keep investigating, be a spiritual investigator, keep questioning it, shine the bright light of truth into its face and keep interrogating it just like a criminal. It will make up all sorts of lies to defend itself, even play bad cop/good cop to catch it out, this criminal doesn't belong in a prison but to be set free, that you your true self will be free also.

You Are No Sinner

Always remember, you are a mistaken identity as long as you identify yourself as the ego mind and its story, you will never know of the love that is bubbling within you, waiting to be discovered like a seed waiting to grow and in this growth you will be set free—the truth as they say, will set you free.

Religion will teach you that you are a sinner and need to be forgiven by an outsider called a Saviour, it will teach you that you must get on your knees and beg for his forgiveness.

Well I'm here to tell you that you are no sinner, you have never been a sinner so stop acting like one, stop acting like a little child that has done wrong, as if big daddy is looking down at you, this is poison to you and this poison is fed to you every Sunday or whatever day.

If there is such thing as a Sin it would have to be when you are off Centre, as the New Testament sin means, to be 'off the target', and as I have already said if your target is God or your true SELF, you can never miss, so sin is only when you believe you are the ego mind body, with this belief you are missing the Whole point, so most of those who push this sin belief, are actually the biggest sinners their very selves, that is in the real sense of the word and its meaning.

So there is no one that can sin, its just another label to attach to your ego and therefore have something to work towards, a new path. It doesn't really matter, the ego will be there to own it, it will take full control and never let you go, it will keep you as long as it can on this new adventure.

This truth can be dangerous to the mind that is not ready to hear it, it will try to control others using it, this is what happens when one takes half hearted truth and tries to sell it to the sleeping ignorant buyer.

In the truth that you are there is no longer buying and selling, there is no longer anything to buy or sell, it was always free, just there waiting for you to take it.

The many who are desperately searching for this truth will travel the world over to find it, they will pay anything for its supposed priceless knowledge, hoping to gain its wisdom for their very selves

Yes, if there's any that are under grace they may see behind this smoke cloud of trickery, but also those who keep in the NOW and continue questioning everything, not in a cynical way but as the spiritual investigator as I have said earlier, they too will find the treasure that was always within.

Be the watcher from the inner tower, watching always what the mind is getting up to, after time you will automatically know that you have been fooled time after time. But do this as a game and as I have already said, don't take it all serious, you are just watching an illusion, the same as seeing in the desert on the hot sands, an illusion of water or oasis in the distance.

To make the game more fun, when listening to others, see if you can catch them out on their neurotic behaviour, listen to their life story being told, but do this in compassion. Remember they are the sleepwalkers, they are under the spell of their illusion, to point this out to one who is sleepwalking is not a very good idea if you don't want an aggressive retaliator, so be kind.

Sons and Daughters

God has not many Sons, but only One

ACIM

Many are led to believe that this God in the sky has only one true Son, that we can only be saved by and through this one Son, but the truth is we are all Gods Sons, or Daughters. There is nothing outside of this God, the only thing that makes one believe that they're outside of this God is the ego mind. As I have said this is too easy for the ego, it needs to make you feel that you deserve to be part of this family of God, it wants to keep you within its hard to get story.

It again wants you to stay on the narrow path to nowhere, because that's the only place it will ever lead you, nowhere, you will forever be waiting for the return of Gods Son, forever and forever . . . waiting.

Realise that you don't have to wait for anyone, I'm here to tell you that the waiting that you were lead to believe is here, NOW, *you are the second coming!*

You were lost and NOW you are found, you were lied to by the establishment, you were lied to by the ego that was conditioned by the establishment. It's time NOW to Realise you don't need anyone or anything to bring you to your inheritance, it was always there but you just never knew how to take it. You always expected someone else to give it to you, this is making yourself a beggar, a beggar who's begging for his own treasure, a treasure that you always had but never went within to claim.

The ego is always going to be the beggar, it is never satisfied, even if it could find the truth it still won't be happy. The truth will never sink within, it will always remain on the surface, the ego just doesn't want to find the truth, it is completely jealous of the truth, it doesn't want to be in second place, it just wants to be the centre of your very being.

This ego who wants to be the centre will make all sorts of wonderful stories to make you believe that it has found the truth, and therefore will leave you alone, but how could it ever leave you alone, when the ego, the illusion, is who you have made yourself to be?

There are those who like to declare their Enlightenment, they will tell you that they are Awakened and will go out and try to Awaken all those around them. There is nothing wrong with this of course but there is no one who can ever Enlighten another, there is also no one that has ever been Enlightened.

Most of those who have or apparently have disappeared into this pure Being, usually keep it all to their SELF—its just accidental that they may become teachers or Gurus—but they will always tell you that they have nothing to give you, that you are wasting your time if you ever do want something from them.

So where does this leave one? Well as I have said if you just stop the search, watch the mind and question everything that comes up from it, you will soon realise that you are not the mind or ego, there is nothing to be done except to be who you truly are, and in this is done by doing nothing.

Yes this is really the lazy mans way to Enlightenment, you see, it's really funny when you start to see it all this way. Take out the seriousness of the so called search and all you will ever do is just laugh and laugh.

Well, they do say that laughter is the best medicine, when the realisation has happen that's all one can really do is to laugh.

Every time that doubt arises just laugh at it, you now know that it's just a big game hosted by one big ego trying to get your attention, imagine this so called ego mind being your best friend, would you put up with it? Of course you wouldn't, you would want to run for the hills.

It's time to fall in Love with your SELF, then you can truly share this genuine love with all others. No longer being the parasite trying to get what it can from the other, to fall in love with your SELF is what you are here for, you didn't make the decision to come here to beg and borrow, you came here to experience this wonderful world that you made, so its time for you to really get to know your SELF.

We are told from day one to always think of others, put others before ourselves, but how can we honestly do this when we don't even know who we truly are ourselves? You can only share what you already know, if you don't know who you truly are then you have nothing whatsoever to share with anyone.

You are only a puppet then, the puppeteer being your ego, pulling the strings, the pull on your heart that you believe to be love is nothing but the ego pulling the strings of your very soul, it's time to cut these strings and truly live as you were meant to.

But again who is going to cut these strings? Well again the strings are only another illusion, the detective has again caught the menacing ego masquerading as the illusional puppeteer.

You see, all these ideas I present to you are only metaphors, all they do is point you to where the light is shining. Don't get caught up in the words I'm describing or trying to describe, after all I'm no expert, I haven't done a PhD in any of this, a PhD in fact would only take you further away from what IS.

All this is very innocent, even a child knows it, but then, he is conditioned to not know it and of course the ones doing or passing the conditioning onto him, have themselves been conditioned. This is why we need to wake up, wake up and see what really is going on around us. When we at least see what's going on in this sleepy little world, we then can at least make our life much more pleasant, not because we are trying to find something out there, but because we have now discovered that there is nothing out there that could ever make us totally happy. We now have at least a small morsel of

what is to come, and what is to come is going to put you right out of your mind, you have to be right out of your mind to ever see this inner Being, you will also never see it with just your own eyes, that is, the eyes in your head, you can only see it with inner vision, inner intuition.

14

Just Be Who You Are

So what are we going to do about this friend that we can't get rid of? Is he or she really our friend at all?

Well like any friend who treats us like this we just have nothing to do with them, we leave them in their own world, we don't let them drag us into their world of illusion that they have created, a world that is poison, a world that won't let one live to their full potential.

This is what the ego has been doing to you, it has kept you away from truly experiencing your true nature, it has been sucking the very life out of you. Yes it has caused you misery and all because of your own creation.

So what can we do? Create another identity, another ego? No we don't create anything, we are already who we are created by no one, we are creation it SELF.

What could be more simple than just being who you are? All you have to do is drop the crap that has been clinging to you, let it go, why would anyone want to cling to crap. The thing is that you have been so used to this crap that you can't even smell it or taste it, you have taken this crap and moulded it into who you are.

It is time for a spiritual enema, to rid you of all that crap you have accumulated, the more you allow your true Self to enter the more crap will start to leave you. God or Consciousness will only enter in its fullness when you are empty of all that crap.

Just like when one is constipated they feel heavy and dull, when they have shifted the build up crap in their body they now feel light and full of energy.

I'm sorry for using this crappy metaphor but that's really what is happening to you, your whole life is full and dull, there is no room within you for true happiness, true Love—it's taken over by this crap you believe is you.

Everything is Consciousness expressing its SELF, even our crappy life, but the difference is that you can either live your life the way it always has been, or you can drop all this crap and live a life free of this build up of crap; it's really your choice and of course you really don't have a choice, while you are still under the illusion that this mind body full of crap, is you, any decision you make is going to be a crappy decision.

Again as I keep saying you cannot do anything, all you can do is watch it, watch the crap, smell it, taste it, then let it go where it came from, and that's the mind body, remember you are not the mind body, you are pure Being, pure Consciousness. In Consciousness I mean an Awareness, an impersonal Consciousness not of the self conscious mind body.

In this impersonal Consciousness we are above the mind body, here we walk above the waters, above the crap that the world collectively is made of.

Just like a rose growing through cow dung, its beauty arises above towards the sun, towards life, its time now for you to grow above all the crap and break through to fullness of your true Being, to your true beautiful Self in Consciousness.

15

Sandcastles

When we speak of our SELF in Consciousness, don't forget that this SELF is ONE, there's no other, we are all this pure Being, being you, being me.

There is no separation we and everything else is ONE, there is no boundaries, no fences, the only thing that makes it seem separate is the mind. Of course to a degree, the mind must see things as separate, so as to live here in this world. We are like children making our sandcastles on the beach. We all have a different shape to our sand-castles but they are all made of the same sand, when the day comes to an end we all knock our sandcastles down and then there is no difference, all there is now is the beach as it was.

Everything is like the sand of Consciousness, we are built from it and we co-create our own world from it also. The difference is we believe we are the sandcastles that we have built, when we die we want to take it with us, for this reason we believe in all sorts of belief systems that will support this belief we have, this becomes our crutch. It keeps us and our beliefs supported, we defend it, we even have wars and kill each other over it, when all we are doing is fighting over each others sand-castles. Well I suppose it is fun knocking down others sandcastles but these sandcastles mean much more to us than just sandcastles on the beach, their our whole life, without them we feel we are nothing.

One good way to see if you are addicted to your sandcastles, is to knock one down and see your reaction, it may be a belief or it could be a favourite food that you like, just try to go without it for a week or so and again be the investigator, take note of how you are feeling towards this sandcastle that you have knocked down. You may find yourself quickly rebuilding it, in some cases you may rebuild it even stronger than before, again take note.

Keep a diary of your castles or beliefs and keep trying to do without another and then another, of course there is nothing wrong with our castles that we build, its just when we are unconscious of them and don't realise that they have a very strong hold on us. By continuing to be vigilant we start to become more Conscious of our little world we have build around us, we also become conscious of everyone else's addictions to their own castles, all we are doing is being the detective, just taking notes and comparing notes with ourselves and others.

We are now becoming experiential in our higher consciousness of thought, we are still using the mind but now we are using it as a tool and not letting it use us as a slave.

We are now becoming more alert and we are starting to notice more and more of what is happening within ourselves, and as well as others, right now it is a good thing to be aware of others around us, as other mind bodies also will keep us in our slumber of unconsciousness, again, be alert and keep being the detective, after all its all elementary dear Watson.

16

Christ Consciousness

L ike a good detective we have to keep questioning the suspect, we have to keep him cornered, and catch him out every time he lies, this is what the ego will try to do, and remember it's a complete expert at manipulating and lying, it will not give in without a fight.

On top of all this remember also that its not even real, it's the greatest show on earth, and all the time you have been the act in the centre ring, while it was the ringmaster with its whip, commanding you to do your tricks, that the ego or ringmaster has taught you. It's time for you now to take the whip and be your own Master, its time to make the ego your slave, well at least an illusionary slave. Like the story of Jesus chasing the money changes out of the Holy Temple, we need also chase the ego that has brought and sold us nothing but misery and lies, then we are left with the most Holy of Holies, we are now ONE with the father or Consciousness.

Just as Jesus became the Christ we also need to transcend the mind body, go under the waters of purification, to die and be renewed as our own inner Christ.

The Christ Consciousness is our mediator between Heaven and earth, we now more or less have made contact, we now transmit and receive through intuitional messages that are going to and from Heaven, the ego now is slowly dissolving in the background of the now purifying mind.

The mind is now becoming our friend, it is becoming our tool no longer dictating to us, this is where many go wrong in trying to make the mind a total enemy, where in reality the mind is neutral, its just a tool, like any tool you can build destruction or you can build peace.

So, who is using the mind? Where is the information that comes through the mind coming from? When we go within to our very Being, into the silence, we are no longer under the power of the ego, what emerges now is pure thought, it is coming from the deep well of our very SELF, our very Consciousness.

Remember that in this so called well that we all drink from, there isn't a well for you and another for me, its just ONE well. Through intuition we draw from this well, this is why most deep Spiritual profound messages that we read or hear from scripture or channelled directly through mediums are always very similar. No matter what scriptures you read from you will always find the truth being pointed to, the sad thing is that some of these scriptures over many years have been tampered with, this has caused them to lose their flow of spiritual meaning. I believe that even though this has happened, still those who read them with spiritual discernment will get the point of the message being conveyed to the reader. To develop this means of drawing from the well of inner Being, we can go within and find that place of silence, by just watching the mind when under control of the ego and seeing it for what it is, just an illusion. When this silence becomes totally you, when you are taken completely over by its beauty, its Love, you will from there know that what is being drawn into you is God speaking to you, you will Know this when it happens, believe me you will Know.

This recognition from within is like for the first time in your apparent life recognising a friend that you completely forgotten—it is all coming back to you—you now are starting to realise who you have always been, but through the mistaken identity of believing you were the mind body, you have forgotten your True SELF.

You have been deceived by this parasite that has been living its false life through you. It's time now to cut the umbilical cord that has been attached to you, of course you will only be able to cut this cord with a spiritual scalpel, you will never be able to cut it with the mind.

Remember the mind right now is still under the power of the false mind or ego, again you must go within and find that inner sanctuary, from there you will obtain this spiritual scalpel, the scalpel of truth will now overpower the ego mind.

There is really only ONE power, this power that the ego thought it had was only an illusionary power.

Jesus said "I of myself can do nothing without the Father, He does the works through me." Jesus of himself was only the mind body organism, but he knew the secret that is within, a secret that is revealed to those who have been within and tasted the pureness, the essence of pure LOVE. This is your Spiritual scalpel that will sever the illusionary cord that has held you in its prison.

You don't need to do anything to cut this cord, just by allowing what is within to shine through, the light will on its on accord sever the hold that the ego had on you. At this time it will feel like an internal war going on but don't forget that there is really only ONE power, this war that you are feeling is just the illusionary ego kicking and screaming, let it kick and scream, it is only desperately trying to get your attention, after all you have been giving life to it, feeding it all your neurosis. When you finally start to live in the NOW, no longer in the past or the imagined future, your neurotic life will begin to lose its flavour, its smell, its taste which was all crap, your new life NOW, will be as a beautiful flower that grows through the crap and holds its head up to the heavens, releasing its beautiful perfume which it shares to all. This inner perfume is the truth of your Being, it will attract to its SELF others who will notice a difference in you, and through compassion you will hand over to the other your torch of Enlightenment, of course this is all not to be taken literally, this is just how I see it, when you begin to see it you will then have your own metaphor or pointers to share with others, maybe even write a book?

But of course you don't have to do anything, everything is just how it should be, everything is just Being, being Being, if you want to share this with others, then its Being, being shared, if you don't, then its Being, not being shared, there is no right or wrong in this sharing or no sharing.

The collective Consciousness is slowly rising throughout this planet, the old idea of religion is slowly fading, the dark ages tried hard to keep the light away from us, organised religion is also trying its best to put us back to the dark ages, the coming of Heaven on earth is near.

Remember that everything that I say here is not to be taken as gospel truth, also remember that there is no one to know anything and no one to do anything, there is just Being—if anything is going to happen it will be because of Being, nothing to do with you or me.

17

There is No One To Be Enlightened

The ideas that I have shared with you are only my ideas arising from Being, if they work or not for you it will only be because of Being, not working or working, there is nothing you can do to be Enlightened because again there is no one to be Enlightened.

There has never been anyone Enlightened, so, what about the Buddha you ask? Well what about him? There was never a Buddha, there was Gautama who supposedly lived about 500BC but he wasn't Enlightened, there was a recognition of Being but recognised by no one, Gautama wasn't there to be Enlightened. The story of the Buddha being Enlightened is just that, a story, the mind body organism of Buddha, you and I are just a story, its just Being being a story. All there is is Consciousness playing games, we are within and part of that game, we are Consciousness playing hide and seek. Consciousness hides and we seek, we organise this seeking and call it religion, this is just another game of hide and seek. But all the time Consciousness is inviting us to be seen, its right in front of us, its right within us, in fact its who we are, Consciousness playing you and I.

So, what do we do then? Like I keep saying, there's nothing, there's nothing to do, there's nothing that can be done, if there is then who is going to do this?

Again we can play the part of the detective, questioning this who, remember its all a game, you can take it serious or you can just play with it, its all up to you, its your story.

Of course you can always finish the story and play the part of being Enlightened, but don't forget it's still a story, its now just a story of you being Enlightened. If believing this story of being Enlightened makes your apparent life more happy, then isn't that all you really want, to be happy? You see we are all just selfish, we are always trying to find something to make us happy, that includes Enlightenment.

If you want something from Enlightenment you will never achieve it, but when Enlightenment is allowed without you doing anything then there is just Being, being Being. It all just goes around and around in circles, because while we are wanting Enlightenment we are never going to get it, we can never get it because we are it, we are pure Being, again paradox after paradox after paradox and so the game goes on.

This all sounds very frustrating to the mind, it just won't accept this, this is why this so-called Enlightenment is seen by many to be so hard to achieve, and as I keep alluding to you, there is nothing to achieve, there is nothing you can do to achieve anything. Now this is a good time to bring the investigator back to the picture or story, why am I feeling frustrated? What is this ego mind doing to me? Am I the ego mind? Who is the I that I am thinking is me?

Do you see the mind going around and around? It's just not happy with this simple answer, and don't forget that this answer isn't the answer to what IS, because there is no answer to what IS, there is just Being, being Robert and whatever Robert says is just Being giving you an answer from Being. Whatever that answer is, be it right or wrong to you, its all still Being, being right or wrong.

You may have noticed that I don't use other belief systems to describe this Being that we are discussing, this is because whatever others have shared doesn't make it any closer to the pure Source of Being. Even the so-called pointers that we us to point one to what IS, we have made into a concept and therefore is never going to be what IS.

So! There's nothing to do, so why even continue reading any further? Well, it doesn't really matter, you don't even really have a choice, there is no one to make the choice, there is just this mind body appearing in Consciousness, whatever way it goes. It is all to do with the programming and conditioning, its nothing to do with you being Consciousness, Consciousness doesn't need to find its SELF, if you were your true SELF, that is in its pure form, that is before its coagulation of its SELF, and remember even in its coagulation its still Consciousness, then you wouldn't be searching for anything, you are already IT.

18

Become As A Child

I t's just in the form that you are appearing that makes you think you are separate, and need to find your true SELF, to discover this so-called true SELF is like a wave on the ocean that has emerged back to the ocean, there was never a separation, it was just the illusion of separation. As I have already said you can't get rid of the illusion because it's not even there, you formed it through your mind, then your mind brought it to the surface of the ocean and you as the thought that emerged, is believing it is you, this is the illusion.

You don't need to be saved, you don't need to be forgiven, you again, don't need anything, this is where all guilt is dissolved, this is where you drop all these stories that have only stunted your growth and poisoned your innocence, this is where you become as a child again and see the world the way it truly is.

So how should this world really look? It shouldn't look like anything just because we label something, such as a rose, doesn't mean that it is a rose, for what is a rose? You see once we have labelled it a rose we then put the concept of a rose in our memory box, along with the rose we have many other labels, such as colour, fragrance, maybe even the sting it gave us when we got a thorn in our finger. We may also have the memory of the pain from the thorn filed away in our box labelled the rose.

Our whole existence is just that, labels after labels, we are born and then we are given labels from all others around us, be it our parents, teachers, governments, religion and on and on it goes, labels after labels.

But of course we more or less need these labels so as to communicate with each other, but its when we see the rose for the very first time that we then have no label for it, we just see for what it is, pure Being, just pulsating before us in all its beauty, and even this is to label it.

19

Just Words

S o now we have at least some understanding of what it means to be still and Know that I AM God, in this inner stillness is the recognition of being ONE with all. It needs no words, it is just simply a meeting of Consciousness, meeting Consciousness, a reflection of its SELF.

When this reflection of who you are is reflected back to you, there will be an inner Knowing, yes, yes, now I KNOW. This Knowing is not like what we know about knowledge, or a knowing in an intellectual since, it's beyond knowledge, it's beyond intellectualism, it's just simply what IS, recognising its SELF. You see while I am trying to convey to you this inner Being there are more and more paradoxes that will emerge, words are only tools and tools can never be what IS, building words into a beautiful story may seem to have beauty within it, but its still just a story made of words.

We use the word love to describe this inner beauty but what do we mean when we use the word love, what comes to your mind when you hear the word love, again it will all come from your programming and conditioning, you were told when just a child that you must love your parents, that you should love your sister and brother. We are taught also that we need to measure out this love in varying degrees. We are conditioned to hand out more love for our mother or father, depending on our relationship with them, when we grow up and find ourselves a partner we then are told that this person is more special, above everyone else, then again the children come along and then there is a new love that we experience, and then our children become even more loved than anyone else.

This is one reason why I don't like the word or label love, but then if I use another word to replace love then what am I doing, so you can see how words can never be what IS.

So there is really nothing we can say about this inner Being, that we and everything is, again, be still and know that I AM God.

In this stillness we disappear, all that there is left is the background, the silence that was always there, you can call this the I AM, you are not your body, you are not your mind, when we say that I AM, we are not stating what we are, we are just the I AM. To say I am this or that is to step out of the I AM, step out and to be separate, this then makes one into a concept.

20

Come Home

The mind is only the tool that is used to make us believe we are separate so as to survive in this world, the same as our eyes are there so as to see our way through this world, and the same with all our other senses, they're all designed over millions of years of evolution to give us a sense of separation.

There came a period in the history of man where after gaining a higher sense of thought, where he started to question why he is here, who he is, what's it all about, then one night around the camp fire those who contemplated their world around them started to give what they believed to be inner answers. The less intelligent mind would listen in reverence to these story tellers and slowly but surely they organised their stories, and here we are today caught in the web of ideologies and belief systems.

So, are belief systems any good in the realisation of our true Being,? can they ever be any good to us? Well we have to realise that there is no one to be Enlightened, beliefs can be ok if they have something that is useful in our life, or in the help of making a peaceful world.

But in bringing one to ones SELF, no, they are not helpful in that sense, no one can bring you to what you already are. Many scriptures may be helpful in helping one to contemplate on the inner world of silence, but that's where they end. They can be as pointers but not what is pointed to, the menu is useful but you don't eat the menu do you? You eat and enjoy what the menu has ordered you.

Many read the scriptures and feel that they have what the scriptures have described, they believe that they should continue with the scriptures, also the rituals are continually practised. The ritual of going to church every Sunday, the ritual of praying to their God for forgiveness, the ritual of giving ten percent of their wages to the church and a million other rituals.

Why do we need to do all this? Well within us all there is our natural sense of knowing we are not this mind body organism, its like an inner calling to come home, just as the rivers slowly emerge back to the ocean, back to where they came from.

When we go away for a holiday we like to enjoy the separation from our home, but within us we are drawn back home after the holiday is over. The Source is always calling us home, this in and out, here, then gone, but of course in reality all is the Source, the in and the out.

I feel that this is what true love is, it's the calling back to the Source, we feel it within each other sometimes, like when we say we are in love, this is really the source calling. Because in reality everything is the source, we are drawn back in many unusual ways, we can even feel this calling in our favourite sports club, in gangs we feel needed, in organised religion we feel like a family, in sex we can feel a strong calling, in fact in the orgasm we can lose ourselves in each other, this is why we can be so addicted to it. Some even feel this strong magnetism in the act of suicide, a longing to leave the pain, emotional or physical body behind.

I remember when I went through a period of clinical depression I would cry like a little boy missing his mummy and daddy, I would cry out to God "please take me home, I just want to go home." It was just as if I was never meant to be here, I have always had this feeling ever since I was a little boy.

I believe this is what is meant by grace, those who have this strong urge to return home but instead of letting worldly things adopt this urge, they disappear into their home while their still in the mind body, in that disappearance there is a Realisation of being ONE with all that there IS.

I must remind you again, don't take any of this literally, and again I must remind you, there is nothing you can do and there is nothing that needs to be done, everything is perfect just how it is, everything is Being and this story in front of you is Being also, just Being, being Being.

21

Back To The Stew

G oing back to the metaphor of the stew where everything within the stew is one with the stew, to believe that one needs to be Enlightened so as to be one with the stew, is like the carrot or the potato wanting to experience this beautiful tasty stew for itself, when in fact it is the stew, it is the taste of the stew—without the carrot or potato the stew wouldn't be the stew. Everything is the stew, everything is Consciousness, even to say this isn't quite right also, for this suggests that there must be things that are separate when there is no separation at all, so you can see again how we can get all stuck and sticky when we try to describe this indescribable Being.

So here we are in the same predicament as the potato and carrot within the stew, we are thinking we are separate and wondering how on earth can we be One and experience this Oneness? Again you can't, to experience something you have to be separate from it, if the thing you are trying to experience is part of you its already within your own self experience. This inner Being has always been you, its just because you have always been lead to believe that you are separate from what IS, and for this reason you are trying to claim your Self which you were born into, you are trying to claim what is already you.

In fact there is no you or me, there is only what IS, its only when we focus on our little self that we believe we are separate, its like all the cells that make up our body. There are about 80 trillion cells within your body, now imagine every single cell believing that its separate from the body, you see its only when there is a focus on one point that the illusion becomes our own reality.

In this so called reality that we have made we see ourselves distant from all else, when all the time it was just a thought a speck of energy arising and that thought is who we believe we are, again just like the wave on the ocean believing it's separate from the ocean.

So there's these little mind body organisms that seem to pop in and pop out of what we call existence, they're here and then they're gone, we call this life and death, but the reality (if that's the right word) is that there is no life and death, there is just the appearance of that. Its because we cling to the part we call life and are afraid of the other part we call death, when in fact there is no separation, there is just Being, being Being.

22

Our True Essence

In what we call death there is only a change of molecular structures, nothing is lost for where could it go? Its all happening in Consciousness and Consciousness can't be less or more, if it was possible for one atom to be lost, there would be no existence at all, if that was possible of course.

So its not that we should see ourselves as special and unique in this ocean of Consciousness, for to do so again is to see yourself as separate, if there is such thing as being unique it would have to be Consciousness its SELF, and this is who you truly are. We can make ourselves feel that we are more special than even a cockroach, when in fact we are the cockroach as well, its just an existential wave from who we really are, Consciousness.

Who are we in essence, what is our true nature, we are the Essence and our true Nature is pure Being, the personality we attach to the mind body through our programming and conditioning is so strong that it completely blocks out the reality of our true Essence, its just a puff of energy arising that we call the ego.

So when there has been this Awakening by no one, what now drives one onwards, how does one continue living? Well one continues living the same as always, the only difference is that now there is no ownership of what emerges, it is seen for what it is, just Being, being Being. When one eats, one just eats, there is no thinking gee I'm here eating, or gee I'm here not eating, everything is just spontaneously arising from Consciousness and spontaneously disappearing into Consciousness.

So is one still under conditioning when there has been this apparent Awakening? Well yes in a way, but now the conditioning is seen for what it is, just conditioning. If there is conditioning that Now is seen as something from the past, that has been a hindrance to our so called life, then these will by its own invention just drop away, there is no more power given to it, its illusionary life is over.

23

The Word God

So do we have free will, other than what is from the behavioural conditioning? As long as we believe we are the mind body, we will always be under the dictation of the conditioned mind, even in the so called Awakening state there is still conditioning, for how could we possibly let go of all that really makes us for who we are. We still go by the name that was given to us, we still go to work and do what we need to do, the only thing that really changes is the illusion that we are the mind body and all of its conditioning. What we have picked up in this apparent life and is still useful we still use but now we use them as tools.

There are many who believe that after this so called Awakening, life then is free and easy, or its like a new utopia that has been discovered, well as I said before life still goes on the way it has always been, for myself this so called Awakening was like, Oh my God, that's all it is, and this is where the joke was discovered followed by much laughter.

Yes I suppose life is sort of easier and yes some have described it as Heaven on earth but these are not what Is, this high of inner excitement is what is interpreted as it animates through the mind body organism, the labels we attach to this inner excitement is really the same as the labels we attach to an orgasm. The orgasm pulsates though our mind body labelled as pleasure, if we are with someone, say, someone we love, then we will say that we are making love and this orgasm was the love expressed. What I have been describing throughout, may sound as if there is no emotion involved, that I must be emotionally dead, well of course I do feel emotion, in fact very deep emotion but the only difference now is that its not attached to, or a neurotic emotion with a story attached.

So does the apparent Awakening make one loveless and dry? It does seem that way when the words are not riddled in emotion and feelings. I am no poet or a writer, I don't try to dress up my words just to please the reader who wants to believe that all this is fireworks and one big orgasm. The truth is that it's just a realisation that has been recognized by Consciousness meeting its SELF, yes you could say that it's like falling in love but to use this word conjures up all manner of imaginary past conditionings. This is why I like to try as much as possible to stay away from such words that only confuse the apparent message of what I am trying to convey. So if I had to use words that are close to what we believe this word love to be, I first would probably use the word Oneness, to use the word love one is lead to believe that it's all something to get, something to fall in love with. You see when we think this way about what we call Awakening or Enlightenment, we make this thing that we are trying to achieve separate from ourselves, so what we are missing is that this thing that we are trying to achieve, is already who or what we are, its not separate at all.

So it's like having a lover that you love deeply, it's like going out and trying to find this love in another, when all the time you have forgotten about your true love beside you, your lover that has always been there for you, this could be called if we use the biblical language, spiritual adultery. Using the biblical language again we could say regarding our inner being the Christ, we could say that by looking outside of our SELF we are idol worshipping, worshipping a false God when all along your inner Being is God. But the same as 'love' the word 'God' is also tainted with the past; there are as many beliefs in this word God as there are people on this planet, The God that many hold dear is responsible for millions of people being murdered over many thousands of years. This word God has been claimed by thousands; every one of them believing they own this word and are the truth holders of this word. Of course there was never a God that was responsible, it was the belief of millions who saw their so called God outside of themselves. If these blind people had realised that this God was within everyone and everything, they would have saved much misery throughout history, this concept of God can and has been extremely dangerous in the wrong hands.

So again I don't really like to use the word God, but again also if I have to use a word which points to God, then I would probably use the word ONE, but even this word isn't what IS. You see if you say the word ONE, you experience a calmness but when we think of the word God, there's an inner stirring within the mind, of course this isn't always the case but I think in most cases it would be.

Now, if we change these words around and no longer use the old words from the past with their tainted history, would it change things? Well I have to say no, not necessarily, after a time even these words will begin to take on the same negative vibration. The whole point here is that words are never what IS, but here I am trying to use this medium of words to describe what cannot be described.

24

Nailed To The Body

'm probably the most lazy person you'll ever meet, I'm too lazy to research other works on the supposed subject of Enlightenment, I'm just too lazy to find scientific evidence to back up what I am trying to describe and also I'm not academically bright, so what you read is what you get, or should that be what you see is what you get, the only difference is you can't see me.

The intellect wants to know, it wants to pull everything apart and see how it all works, of course there is a place for this but it will never help you or anyone to enter Awareness, it only wants to pull Awareness apart, if that was possible that is.

If we asked a small child what love was, what Awareness was, what is Oneness, they wouldn't be able to tell you or even give you an answer, unless of course they have already been told what one of these questions should be by an adult. A small child just lives for the day, for the moment, they seem to love everyone around them, even strangers, which can be unfortunately dangerous to the child. The child as yet hasn't learnt to not trust certain people, hasn't learnt to hate certain cultures or skin colour and on and on it goes.

As the bible language says, you must be as little children to enter the kingdom of heaven, this doesn't necessarily mean that you have to be a little child, it means that you must become innocent, see what's really there within you, see what is without all the conditioning, all the second-hand knowledge that you have been feed all your life.

This innocence is what I would—if I have to—call love. Just watch a baby when someone cries in front of it, in most cases the baby will start to cry as well, it's as though the baby is part of the person who is crying, it's beautiful to watch. I don't know the psychology behind this but all I do know is what I have seen and what has become my own inner observation. Most of the time there's an inner intuitive knowing what its all about, there's no need to run out and try to prove it is right or wrong.

This is gong on all the time, we seem to have to prove every single thing, we even have those who are teaching this so called awareness arguing between each other, or between their disciples or fans, which is probably more correct. These fans of the particular teacher will also argue with other fans saying that their teacher is better than yours. You have those who argue either straight forward or subtlety that you're not Enlightened and they are.

This is one reason that I don't go out and declare this to the world, not that there's a need to protect myself from those who do or don't agree but because I now see all Enlightened, I see all as the Divine essence, all I see is a game out there with everyone playing, playing how to find their SELF.

Its like watching a comedy that's even better than Monty Python, its like the parrot sketch where the man who wakes up to the fact that the parrot was nailed to the perch and was not even alive. In this I can see that we are all thinking that we are the mind body and that we are nailed to it, then someone realises that we are not the mind body but everyone who sold us the idea that we are, are trying to convince us that we are this body and also nailed to it.

So here we are thinking we are nailed to the body, or getting of the subject of Python, stuck in the body, we believe that we must transcend the body and be free of the ego to obtain true happiness. This is true in a sense but not completely true. We must realise that we are not the mind body, its like if we had a puppet and the puppet started to believe it was the one pulling the strings, yes we could say that the mind body is an extension of who we truly are, but its certainly not totally of who we are. There I go again in a tar pit of words, trying to deliver to you this message I have somehow obtained from this inner intuitive Being, so what am I trying to say here, well as I have said over and over there is nothing you can do to obtain this Awareness, its just there, it's there all the time, again it's like the clouds that block the sun, the sun hasn't gone anywhere, it's just there. So there is nothing I can give to you that you don't already have, but there it is, the mind just won't except this, it's too easy for the mind, it needs something to cling to—something to get its teeth into.

Why is the mind like this? Well the mind itself isn't at fault, the mind by itself is really neutral, it's just a tool, the ego that we have given life to uses the mind to deliver its lies and again of course, all along the ego is only an illusion of who we believe we are. It may all sound frustrating to one who is trying to find this inner happiness, through being Enlightened, while we are still coming from the mind we will be frustrated, and again its not really the mind but how the mind is being used by the illusionary ego, again the mind is only the tool.

While the mind is under the influence of the ego it will keep delivering us nothing but lies, nothing but frustration, this is where we can, even though there is no one to do anything, go within and just sit in that silence of purification, this silence will purify the mind so as to allow intuitive energy, that is translated through the mind which now is no longer under the influence of the ego. Also when we are under the influence of the mind, now purified, we have to release the mind, because of many life times of programming will still have some residue, that will stick to what comes from within intuitively. This is why many teachers if not all, try to deliver their message in so many different ways, each message has to come through a mind body, so if this mind body, is say a Hindu, it will be usually delivered in the light of Hindu teaching. But all truth has the same flavour about it, if any teacher offers you something to be obtained you can guarantee that this teacher isn't or hasn't tasted true Awakening, that is not the mind body of the teacher but the Essence of what is revealed through the teacher.

Really, there is nothing to teach because there is no one to teach anything to, the one who is hearing this message is mostly coming from the mind body, who is wanting something from the teacher, while this is so, what could anything the teacher say, ever change this mind body. Not until this illusion is seen for what it is and all searching has stopped, and one is in total silence, not until you have disappeared will unconditional Love be there to declare its SELF, not until the words of the teacher are reflected back to your true Being will there be any Awakening, Awakening by no one.

Bursting Bubbles

So here I am taking away your hope and pulling the mat from under you, I like to call myself a bubble burster—let's face it, it's as fun bursting bubbles as it is knocking down sand castles. There are those who will like to give you a dream to believe in, they will offer you hope, they will tell you if you keep trying this or that idea, you will one day be Enlightened, but I cannot do that because I have Realised that there is nothing we can do of ourselves, as Jesus said "I can do nothing of myself but the father doeth all the works from within me."

Its only when we become an instrument of God that this inner Being will shine throughout our life, the only way we can become an instrument of God is to surrender to who we truly are, to let go of any ideologies, to let go of everything we ever believed we were. Now see all this accumulated baggage of illusionary rubbish as one giant bubble, and let that inner child within you with all its innocence burst that big bubble, BURST!! Now wasn't that fun?

You can make a little game out of this, when you notice the mind bringing up its crap, just see it all as one big bubble and again, BURST!! You will, after a while, start to notice this ego mind arising in others, but don't go around trying to burst their bubbles, you won't be very popular, but still you'll be entertained. So is it right to go around laughing about others ego's, well if you laugh at yourself first, then why not, after all its just an illusion but don't forget that this illusion is very important to most and many will retaliate, if their ego is threatened in any way, so again be careful.

This world we have made is controlled by the ego, this world when there has been an apparent Awakening can seem like an alien planet, this is what I experienced when after the disappearance I apparently went through. The world around me for a time seemed to be asleep and acting crazy, or was it me acting crazy? Yes it was so confusing at first, but then I started to tune into this inner Being. It was like going to another planet and everything being different to what one is so used to.

This humour I carry on about was full on, I would even see the funny side of so called serious stuff on the television, of course I wouldn't tell anyone, so many secrets need to be kept from the sleeping planet, after all Jesus got crucified for blabbing too much.

It's true that if anyone comes forward and reminds this sleeping world that they are sleeping, they will be put in the too hard basket or the loony bin. Many times I wonder who really are the crazy ones, is the so called normal who spend their whole life trying to be someone, trying to find happiness in all sorts of ways, in a new home, a new lover, a new position at work, are they the ones who must climb the corporate ladder shoving everyone else below them.

Or are the so called sane ones, the ones who have Awaken to this whole circus and don't need to better themselves, don't need to find happiness, don't need to do anything to be more than they already are. These are the ones that society doesn't want, they are no good for the economy, they're not materialistic enough, they're too Awakened to be fooled, and the society as it is, can do far better without them. This is the sad fact that we have got ourselves into and any turning back will be only seen as backward evolution.

So how did we get ourselves into this illusionary trap? Well a long time a ago there was a big bang, if that's how it happened, this big bang was like the opening of an egg. Out from this egg came all that there is, you and I as the human species were potentially within that egg waiting in the silence of no space and no time. Out from this nothingness came the first light of a brand new era, after what is called time this light became pure energy bubbling with excitement, like an orgasmic pulsation, its fluids of coagulated energy which we call matter spurted forward into the vast space that was created by its own immaculate divine will.

This matter was like the clay that the Consciousness of this divine parent played with, moulding for its SELF all kinds of wonderfully inventive play toys. These toys were set in motion by Consciousness to be played with for eternity, just like a perpetual wind up toy.

Because of invisible strings or laws that were placed by Consciousness everything worked together in harmony, it was a beautifully constructive mobile toy. Of course this is not scientifically true but lets just stick to the metaphor for now.

So within this egg and of the egg its SELF was pure Consciousness, pure Awareness, pure Love, and from this egg after an innumerable time measure you and I, hello! Well here we are, . . . but who are we, why did all this happen and what's the whole purpose. Well really there is no answer to these questions, you your SELF created all this, so lets ask our SELF the question, who are we. From the perspective of the mind body organism, we believe we are this body and everything is happening out there within the Cosmos, but if we are the body then where are we within the body, no matter how hard you try you will never find a you there.

So if we are not in the mind body where are we, well we are really everywhere, there is no place that we are not. So you see it can all get sticky when we try to even think about it all, the paradox is that we are not the body but also we are the body, for if Consciousness is all that there IS, then there cannot be anything outside of Consciousness.

So why do I say we are not the body if we are all that there IS, well to say that we are the body is only a very small part of the truth, that is if the truth could be separated, again another paradox. So using the analogy of the light bulb and the electricity, again we are believing we are the light bulb that is giving of the light, now this has truth in it also but the whole Truth is that the life is really the electricity, for when the light bulb no longer works, it has come to its end, and another light bulb is given light too by the ever continuing electricity. Also every other light bulb that is believing themselves to be separate, are all giving their light because of this ONE energy. We could say that this energy is Consciousness, for it is because of Consciousness that everything is what it is, mind bodies so call die and other mind bodies replace the mind bodies that have given way to new mind bodies, and so it all goes on and on.

Just like the Christmas lights with all the beautiful colours of the rainbow, each with their own character and design, so we are also, but also just as the light bulbs on their own cannot give their beautiful light, so we also as the mind body organism have no life without the life force of Consciousness.

26

Consciousness

S o then, what is this Consciousness that is so talked about, well there's probably a million different ideas of what it is and what it isn't, so I may as well make my own version up.

First of all this Consciousness cannot really be described, like the Tao which cannot be named, but lets have a go anyway. Well I feel that Consciousness is like an Awareness, it's Aware of what IS, not itself because this makes it dual, there's Consciousness and there's something outside of Consciousness being Aware of itself, again words, sticky words.

We as the mind body organism are aware of our surroundings and ourselves as the mind body, this self awareness is more or less tied to the mind body—it doesn't see past the mind body—there is no comprehension of what is beyond, it is like it's nailed to the mind body and in a way it is. This self awareness is of the ego with all its programming and conditioning, so the whole awareness is in this bundle of energy that we believe is who we are.

As I described using the light bulb analogy, the bulb is thinking its separate from the Source, or electricity, this is similar to the mind body organism, through its self conscious, believing its self again to be separate, as you would guess we are more than just this body.

Now all this intellectually, sounds as if all we need to do is just say, well ok then I am everything, simple! Now this will not do, for the reason that it has only been known through the mind body self conscious, which can never get it, can never truly Know.

Many who have read books on this subject think yea, I get it and off they go on their merry little way. But always in this situation it just doesn't seem to last, they are back again when something in their life disturbs their new found Consciousness, they are thrown back into the illusionary mind body ego and off they go again searching for their illusive dream.

Like dreams, we have beautiful dreams but we also have nightmares, but still they're just dreams, this is also how we are in this self conscious ego world, we are caught in our own dream prison. I suppose its like me showing you a map of where a beautiful town is, you can study the map for years, you can even look at the beautiful pictures and then say, yes I know all about it now, I know it's beauty, its so wonderful. This is in a way the same as Self-Realisation, thinking one knows when all along one knows nothing and in a way this is so funny, because really there's nothing to know, there is just the "Oh, I see Now," and in that Now, you have really discovered what was there all along. In that Now moment of no moment, the Heavens open, the clouds are gone, the fuzziness of what IS, is now full clarity.

But there is no one to witness this except its Consciousness, it's SELF, Consciousness is reflected back to its SELF, just as the moon shines upon the calm waters of a lake, the moon within the calmness is reflected back to its SELF. We are that lake, but because the waters are so disturbed by the mind, Consciousness cannot be seen for what it Is, it cannot be Realised from within, it cannot be reflected back to its SELF.

We can enter this calmness through meditation but meditation itself will not bring us any closer, its when we leave meditation from within and dissolve into our true Being, completely naked, without any help from the outside world and its techniques, the techniques can only take us so far, then we drop them, and enter Heaven alone in Oneness.

27

Remember, Remember, Remember

I f none of this makes any sense to you, well, it doesn't really matter, it doesn't matter if you get this or not, as I keep saying there's nothing to get, you are already it. But like most people they do want something to at least work with, and I'm not really going to give you anything to work with, but that doesn't mean you can't play with the things I have spoken of, just try to see it all as a game, the game of life where there's no losers or winners, just the game.

If we keep this in mind we will have less chance of being too serious about it all, just keep playing the game of catching yourself out. When you find yourself drifting back to the ego desperately trying to work it all out intellectually, just stop and let it go, then have a little laugh at how easy you are drawn into this mind play, how easy it is to be fooled by this friend of yours that you have known all your life.

Remember, remember, remember, that there is no such thing as being Enlightened. Give the search up, and just put your feet up and relax, realise that you are already there and feel the peace within. When you do relax and give in, as they say your head is already in the tigers mouth, so what can you do, but to just yield to the what IS, surrender, there's nothing you can do anyhow. There . . . now isn't that better, at last its all over . . . at last you're home.

I suppose I should have left those few paragraphs to the end of this book, but then would it really be over? Or would you just carry onto the next book, the next story of how to be Enlightened. Well this is what most will be doing.

The whole thing is that we are addicted to the path itself and as with all addiction we got to keep the supply up, so there's the demand and there's the supply, you keep demanding and all the Gurus will keep supplying, so what am I doing, well supplying you nothing. Now even though there's nothing here for you, the ego will still want this nothing, it can even get hooked on this nothing, well what a drug, a drug that does nothing, but would it ever sell, you bet.

But just in case I'm wrong, I'll keep going on anyhow, don't forget there's nothing here right or wrong, there is just what is, just words coming from somewhere within me and you are there probably sitting reading them and thinking "what a clown." Well you would probably be right, I do feel like a clown sitting here preforming for you, writing these jokes and trying to weave them together to entertain you, yes this is the biggest show on earth, everything is happening here as is everything is happening everywhere. Really we are all clowns here with our make up on, our persona or mask, in fact most of us wear a different mask wherever we go. We have a mask for working, for our wife or husband, our kids, just about everything and all along we are fooling ourselves thinking we are the mask. The ego is our invention its not our true individuality, we are born in pure Being, we then through the already programmed entities, take in the information they feed us and this then becomes our programming, we then hand this down to the next generation and so it goes on and on. Also our idea of what love and happiness is because this also was handed down to us from a world full of neurotics, we never really live our life at all, we are living a life that we are programmed to be.

28

The Inner Lover

So if we are not the programmed mind body that we thought we were, then who are we and what should we do? Well again nothing, you only have to be who you are, when you see a tree, see a tree, don't see the tree through eyes that have already been programmed. See the tree for the very first time, like a child you will see more than what you have ever thought was there. When we see this tree we straight away see what we have been told what to see as this tree, we say yes this tree is green or this tree is an oak tree or a lemon tree. Of course we need to use this language or labels to describe the tree to others but within ourselves we can see the tree as a tree, we then will see everything around us as if for the very first time.

You see we are so conditioned by labels that we forget what we did see as a child. I remember when I was a child everything was so fantastic and so enchanting, because I was seeing all without labels, of course labels have their place in the world of communication but that's where it should end. To hold onto that pure innocence is to live a life in individuality, our individuality is pure Being, the tree itself is pure Being, it is shining its individuality through your individuality and all this individuality is ONE.

Unlike the so called individuality we have with our false selves the ego, our true individuality is our so called SELF Awareness, it is not contaminated by billions of years of evolution and many thousands of years of conditioning.

Throughout the day we have little glimpses of no mind, we may just go into a dreamlike state, sort of like a daydream. In that few seconds we are not here, we don't feel the mind body we are just lost in that moment of no moment. Also in sex when we are in total orgasm with each other, we lose ourselves for just a few seconds, there is no me, there is just a disappearance into total pure pleasure, this pleasure of Oneness is soon forgotten and is sought after time after time, it becomes an addiction, a beautiful experience but still an addiction.

Many also try to reach this inner freedom through drugs. Drugs can give you this sense of freedom from the mind body perspective but its all just tricks of the mind, giving you a false sense of inner security more or less. We all go through this life asleep trying always to find something to relieve our inner wanting. As I have already said, this inner wanting is not wanting anything, its just our inner Being calling us home.

When we listen intuitively to this inner voice—a voice that we have never really forgotten—this is the voice of our inner Lover, this inner Lover is our first love from right back from our first glimpse of light from the primeval egg of Consciousness. This love story is a love story where everyone of us is in love with the same and only Lover there is.

While we are still asleep we will continue trying to find this Lover in just about anything you can imagine, and again so many believe they have found this love in another, they will cling to this person, they will even murder for this person or even murder the person themselves.

Hitler helped to murder about 6 million people for the love of his country and ideologies he believed in, and yes this was all in the name of love, a false love covering and hiding the true Love from within all of us.

As I keep saying there's nothing we can do to obtain this so called Awakening, but with that said I do feel that for those who are under the grace of their true Being, at least a little push can't hurt.

So if I had to give one a prescription I think I would give them a prayer, not really a prayer where we are after something like so many do, they take their shopping list to God begging him to fulfil their greedy wishes. This prayer is what I call a genuine prayer, its really you praying to your SELF, that is to your so called higher Self, you're not praying to a separate being and hoping for this being to answer your prayers.

As I have told you earlier in my story when there was this disappearance into total Being, my prayer to this God that I knew somehow was right within me, was as a child crying for his mother or father, it was a heartfelt prayer, just crying to be home in the arms of the ONE who truly Loves me.

I suggest once you have questioned this self you always thought was you, after you have caught this impostor out over and over again and have come to the point in your apparent life that you just can't do anything. Then from here just surrender, truly surrender. In this surrendering just relax either in a chair or lay down on the bed, then just call out from deep within your heart, this must come from an area deep within. If you're sincere—and you must be sincere—then your calling may bring you to the edge of your true Divinity. There you will Know, believe me you will Know, from there you may just be able to peep through the curtain, in this Divine inner space you may just see who is peeping through the curtain at you.

To get to this stage of truly surrendering you cannot fool yourself in believing you are there when in fact you are not, its like when someone dies that you really love and you are wishing they were back with you again, you just cannot pretend this stuff. This is why throughout the book I keep saying to realise that you cannot do anything, this hope of no hope is what will bring you to this stage of truly pining to be home, a home that you truly Know of and can feel throughout your whole Being.

So if this prayer is genuinely asked from deep within you, if tears flow in this longing to be home then just let them flow. As I said keep your inner eyes on the split in the illusionary curtain, see the split in the curtain becoming wider and wider, just keep heading for the gap in the curtain, if any thoughts arise which they will, just let them go, don't take hold of them, they're not yours to take hold of. In this what I'll call mediation, but don't take any notice of the label, we will feel the mind body becoming restless, it will try to put up a fight to bring you back to where it wants you, it will be like a spoilt child who wants you to play with it, it will get very jealous when you ignore it. So for his reason it might be a good idea for you to make a quiet time when you can relax and let go.

In this quiet time the ego is not invited so it's best to leave it outside, for there is no room for it within you, it will only try to steal the show. It will try as hard as it can, and always remember, remember, remember, that this little jealous child isn't even real, it's the illusion of all illusions, but it's still there in our mind so we will see it for what it is, not what it wants us to believe.

I must say here that this prayer must not come from the outer mind of clinging, if there is clinging, that is to cling to what the prayer is pointing to, then that's all you will ever have is another emotional attachment to cling to. As I keep saying and I will keep saying is that you, the mind body can do nothing, absolutely nothing. So this is why I say, you have to go within naked, even more naked than the day you were born, this will be you who hasn't yet tasted from the tree of knowledge of good and evil, that is your pure innocence, your pure Being.

You don't have to know what these are, this innocence, this pure Being because you can never know what they are because you are that already, so all you have to do is be your SELF, and to be your SELF you don't have to do anything except to be still, to feel that stillness deep within and rest in that stillness.

So try to forget about taking anything that I have said literally, again the mind, because it cannot absorb this will want to understand it, so we need to forget about the words but go where the words are pointing, as they say go towards the light.

Whatever will happen will happen not because of you doing anything but just because of the silence meeting the silence, and

in this kiss, will be the true Love of your life. It will be like the second coming of the Christ but within, in this beautiful meeting of Oneness, heaven now will be established here where you are, on earth. There are probably thousands of techniques of so called ways to obtaining Enlightenment. This, what I am sharing, I don't like to call a technique which is a method, there are no methods to this, there's no final solution. If this so called Awakening happens, it will happen, not because of any method, or anything that I have shared with you.

I have said over and over that you don't need to do anything, I have said over and over that you are already there, that you are it, but still the mind won't believe this. So even though there's nothing one can do, at least quieting the mind and entering that place of no place within you, there if anything is going to happen will happen.

Another way that you may like to experiment is to start at the relaxing stage I spoke of earlier, now just let yourself drift out from every direction, not just upwards because there's no such thing as upwards, Now again let your self expand in all directions, expand further and further outwards. Now feel every single cell in your body drifting apart from each other, if you start to panic a little just stay there in the silence and feel the Love that is bubbling within you.

When you are ready keep expanding outwards, expanding, expanding outwards. Now imagine you are seeing all the stars and the planets, keep drifting past these planets, feel the coolness and feel the silence of space, look around you and realise that this is all you, you have created all this, and all this that you have created is also you, there is nothing that isn't you.

If you feel that you are starting to get restless then just let yourself come slowly back to the body, go through all this in reverse until you are there lying down on your bed, don't just get up and move but just stay there for a few minutes until you feel you are completely back in the body, just breath in and breath out and open your eyes.

This prayer and meditation isn't something I read about or learnt, it is just what I went through before I apparently disappeared into Oneness, I never planned to do this it just spontaneously came about without any thought on my behalf. Because this is experimental or something that I cannot name that happened within me, all I can share with you is what happened.

This may not be any help to you, or then again it could be what is needed to just push you over the edge of the cliff, to plunge into the depths of inner Being. If you have at this stage realised that you are not the mind body, that you are not the ego that has taken your true identity onto itself, if you realise that you are all that there IS, then you are ready to take this plunge. If you are not ready then this plunge will only frighten the hell out of you, in fact there are some that, because they're not ready to swim in this ocean of consciousness, will begin to thrash about, they have fallen into this pure silence but they're not totally ready as yet.

I believe that there are many who have a mental illness such as schizophrenia, who are so close to their true being but because they are not as yet ready they more or less drown in their own Being. The mind is so mixed up that it is like it's being scrambled between what IS and what isn't. These people even start to believe they are God or Jesus, they are right in the metaphorical sense but because of the ego mind being so scrambled this all comes through the mind in total chaos, or what is medically called psychotic.

I remember when I was in a psychotic state I would feel as if I wasn't the body, I was looking down at myself just like I have read about near death experiences, it was if I wasn't in the body but was attached to the body with a cord of some sort, I remember when I had a shave I would look in the mirror and the face in the mirror looking back at me wasn't me, it was so frightening at the time. I think all this came about because of so much emotional pain that I couldn't stand it any more, like I have said all I wanted was to go home, I just felt this deep longing to go to this place that I felt so strongly about.

What I found out after the apparent Awaking was that there is no geographical place that is home, this place that I felt was my home was our true Source, our pure Being. I also found out that I was home all along, all I needed to do was walk through the illusionary door that most of us think is locked; we go throughout our lives trying so desperately finding the illusionary key to open this illusionary door.

> *For every one that asketh receiveth; and he that seeketh*
> *findeth; and to him that knocketh it shall be opened.*
>
> Luke 11:10

As Luke says, for everyone that asketh receiveth, this is the genuine prayer I shared earlier with you, he that seeketh findeth. In this prayer is found the true seeker of their pure Being, this is truly their home, those that knocketh, it shall be opened, to him that comes within and finds that place of pure silence, this pure silence is the door to your true SELF, just the inner recognition is all that is needed to open this door, a door that you always thought was locked.

We Are All One

So now we realise that there is no door, there is no key, there is no path, there is no Enlightenment, there's just you, the real you and you are me as I am you and there's only ONE you. Isn't that fantastic? Like every single person as well as everything else is you, is me. You don't ever need to be anyone famous or anyone that you believe is better than you, because you are he as he or she is you, and again you are me as I am you and we are all together as ONE. Just play around with that thought for awhile, let it really sink in to you.

Yes the old ego will try to jump in and think "Wow, I'm [add name], gee he or she is so famous I must be great also?" You see this thinking is still from the ego's perspective, it cannot comprehend that we are all ONE, for this to the ego means it has nothing to compare itself to, it wants to be better than the rest. But the truth is we are all ONE, and those who are at the top of the list of the greatest, and those at the bottom of the not so great are all equal.

Because of this realisation we see those who are causing grief as part of ourselves, this causes us great compassion towards these people not revenge, after all their a part of us also. Just like cancer cells within the body, its because of these cells not cooperating with the rest of the holistic body that can lead to death of the whole body.

Of course sometimes we need to castrate these people from the rest of society, in order that they won't affect the whole of the collective body, this is also what we try to do with cancer. So here we all are as

ONE collective Consciousness, but it even goes further than that, it goes beyond the Collective Consciousness to Cosmic Consciousness which is beyond anything the mind could even cope with, in fact there is no need to even worry about all this Consciousness stuff, like I said you can never know it, you are it and all you have to do is be it. Don't try to be it but just within that silence I spoke of, in that stillness just rest, this is the Sabbath, the true Sabbath of rest.

You have spent all your life creating this and creating that, creating all these material things that will never last, now in this rest you finish all that you have been creating and rest from all your works. So many have thought of this Sabbath as a day to worship, because of God when he rested from his creation, but this is only the outer teaching. My own church that I joined many years ago, the Seventh day Adventist, strictly adhered to this commandment that was given to the Jews supposedly by Moses. Whenever I would bring up the discussion of the Sabbath no one wanted to hear this deeper side of the spiritual meaning, at least, spiritual to me, they thought that by thinking of such things in a spiritual way as I did at the time was of the devil. They believed that we are in dangerous territory when thinking too deeply about such things as the Sabbath, after all the Sabbath was their main teaching since 1844.

Now I don't bring this up for the reason to pick on the Adventist, my whole point is that too many so called religious belief systems are too fixed on the outer message of their very own teachings, within their own teachings is to be found many signs that point to what IS. There is only one true devil and that's our mind trying to keep us away from truly Knowing our true identity, Consciousness.

The trouble with organised religion is that, its organised, you cannot organise the truth, you cannot wrap it up and package it. Truth is our very Being, it cannot be named it can only be pointed to, it cannot be owned, many religious organisations believe that they alone hold the truth, they believe that if your not in their organisation believing what they teach, then you will never be saved.

This way of thinking is all because of the ego mind wanting to be right, wanting to believe it has something that you don't have.

The sad fact is that most of these people don't even realise that their under the influence of the hierarchy ego mind, pretending to be the one and only way to freedom, or in most cases, heaven. They childishly believe that there is a geographical place in the sky, somewhere where one day they and their loved ones will all meet, they even believe that they will be cuddling lions and tigers, eating fruit such as grapes the size of melons.

All this sounds so wonderful and makes the heart flutter, but its all one big fairy story, its not a heaven in the sky but a pie in the sky story, and millions of people are believing it all. Now of course they can believe what they like but for the genuine so called seeker this will never bring you into total Being, total Love, total Consciousness, these ideas or ideologies will only keep you outside looking in, never really knowing what truth is, that is the inner Knowing, the inner discovery.

The story of Jesus was the Christ within us all personified, when he said such things as "I am the way, the truth, the light" He was telling the truth but he never meant that he alone was these things, but each and everyone of us is also this truth. They have shoved these God men such as Jesus, the Buddha, Krishna and whoever else up high on a pedestal, that no one can reach and those who do openly reach them are seen as crazy, or blasphemers, when all along these very people are the blasphemies themselves. These people are your true anti-Christ, antiBuddha's, anti-Krishna's, they are all against you becoming your true Divinity. They are afraid of those who proclaim their true SELF, this is seen as rebellion and many were and still are killed for proclaiming who they truly are. I tried to talk about this in my own church and was suspected as being crazy, like with the mental illness and all, well I had to be crazy didn't I?

As I have said, I use to be a deacon in the church and after I started to share what I was so excited to share, I was quickly taken away from my position, well you can't have a deacon not believing what the church wants you to believe, now can you? All belief systems are just an excuse formulated by the ego to keep us away from ever Knowing the truth, the truth of or true individuality, an individuality where we are all ONE.

This illusion has been the parasite that has sucked the life out of all of us, it has left us with nothing more than a shell, the kernel of truth has been forgotten long ago. So what is the big deal in the Realisation of who we truly are? Well if there were many more people in the world who have entered their true Being, and have tasted at least, the pure Essence of Love from within and the true happiness that has always been there, then we would be living in a much happier and neurotic free world.

Of course in reality it doesn't matter, everything is perfect just the way it is, it couldn't be any other way, but still it can be also any other way we want, and that will also be perfect, it really doesn't matter. But with that said we still see a imperfect world with many searching for happiness. For those who are searching for true happiness may at least stumble over their SELF, and in that stumble or fall, Realise that it was always there, right within themselves.

So this is really what is behind all that I am trying to say, and as I keep saying that we can't do anything, I say this in a positive way, that which you are after is already within you. By keeping you away from the continual searching I am trying to help you realise that you are IT. I believe in being honest with you and not try to lead you down some mystical path, and make what I have in my apparent life discovered, seem too hard for you to ever obtain, as if myself, is someone far above you.

No this message that I am sharing is just by some ordinary dude, just a simple under-educated academically dumb guy. When you realise that you are not your little life story, you then realise that no matter how many PhD's you have, it will not make any difference to your Realising your true Being. In fact the more educated you are the more you will question this simple philosophy, you will throw up all sorts of arguments to defend your treasured highly educated badge which the ego mind wears so proudly. To be able to even come close to this so called Awakening one must come as they are, nothing attached, no ideologies, no beliefs of any kind, especially the belief that you can be Enlightened.

This is another paradox, as I keep saying you can only give up, and even that you can't do, you can only stop trying and even that you can't do. So when this is seen from within, not with outer eyes but with inner intuition, then and only then it may or may not happen. There are many of us that are like wet wood and there are those who are like dry wood, there are also those who are like gunpowder, these are the ones who only need to hear the truth or read one sign that points to the truth, these are the ones who like gunpowder will ignite into Consciousness, they instantly disappear into their true Being.

Others who are more or less not quite ready can be the so called dry wood, they will need a little more coaxing to bring them to the waters edge, where they can only cross after they have dropped all that they own, and all that they cling to. Then we have those who are like wet wood, no matter what they do they will never be able to drop anything, they are too rich to enter heaven, they cling to too much, which no matter what they do they will never be able to let go. These are the ones who are frantically trying to find happiness outside themselves, these are also the ones who keep the economy going in a big way. You may say well, what's wrong with boosting our economy? Well, of course there's nothing wrong with that, but if you want true inner happiness, you will have to find true happiness first, and like I said you have to drop everything that you have thought brought you happiness, no matter what it is, you must give up all these treasures if you ever at all want to enter your true Being, or if you like, Heaven.

When we have discovered this Heaven within we have also discovered true happiness, true love. We now are no longer after happiness outside of ourselves, instead of now being under the manipulation of the economy, in its supply and demand, we have now come back to the demand and supply. We no longer need to run out and grab everything new that hits the market, just because we are told that we are nothing if we don't. We are also told we are going to be left behind, if we don't keep up with the Jones's.

We now simply buy things because we want to, not because we feel we need to, we are no longer under the voice of addiction telling us over and over in our heads, that we need this or we need that. Also now we don't run out and grab the first man or woman to be our loved one, just because we think we are incomplete without them. We are told by meaningful but neurotic people that if we don't find someone to complete ourselves, that we are going to be left behind, that we are going to be very lonely when we grow old, when in fact these meaningful people are only projecting their own insecurity on to us, they in themselves cannot understand how anyone could ever be happy without someone else.

This love that we are all chasing outside ourselves is just another addiction of trying to find happiness. There are also many trying to find this so called Enlightenment, they believe once they have found it, there will then be happiness for them for the rest of their lives. The thing is you can never find happiness no matter where you believe it to be, if you do find this happiness that you have been after, then you will soon find that there's a flip side to it, the flip side is unhappiness.

True inner happiness doesn't cling to anything, it is happiness unto its SELF, it even accepts what we term as unhappy, seeing that there is no division but seeing it all as ONE energy arising from pure Being. When I speak of this pure happiness from within, in itself to call it happiness isn't really what is, for whatever I call it, that isn't what it is, again words are not what IS. I keep repeating myself over and over again because I don't want you to become addicted to what I am trying to point you towards, not to cling to the signs, the words. The ego mind is very cunning and will find any excuse to cling to something to keep itself alive and kicking.

Addiction and Greed

We again just need to be like the detective questioning everything, even what I am sharing, so to be in the NOW, and not in the past or the so called future: for this is where the ego will try to cling to keeping the illusionary dream alive. Also we must remember not to cling to even all that has been said about not clinging, for even here the ego will try to take control and organise all this to make another path to follow.

There are so many that have worked hard all their lives and have put so much into their work, they will tell you over and over how wonderfully they work. In fact this is all they ever talk about. The work that they do has become their unconscious escape, their life is meaningless without this clinging to the only thing that makes them feel as if they are worth something. In many cases their life at home is no longer satisfying and the only escape into what they believe makes them whole is their work, but what happens when they retire.

So just like any addiction, work can be an addiction also. When these people retire they just don't know what to do, their whole world has come to a stop, their whole story has been interrupted. Many sadly die not long after, their minds craving its fix becomes emotionally torn apart, its just as if they have lost someone dear to them. What they have lost is actually something very dear to them, it's the ego's fulfilment, to the ego this clinging to something like ones job, is really no difference than one who has lost a loved one, it's all the same to the ego mind, but with only different labels attached.

So again here we have someone who believes they have found happiness—if not fulfilment—outside of themselves. This list of outside happiness could fill many books so I won't go into fine details on this matter, but I'm sure you get the point of what I am trying to show you.

Love is also the same as happiness when found on the outside, there is really no difference, again its just the labels and the story of what emotions we are told to apply to these varies labels. Because we are conditioned to believe that or own species is above all else, we then make this label more valuable than say, a job or our car, when really it's no difference to the the ego mind.

So all these emotions that we feel, control our whole entire life, we are nothing without them. Questioning these emotions will have the ego rebelling to protect itself, it will try to do anything it can to stop anyone who has caught it out in its game. There it was all snuggled up to you like a big teddy bear and someone comes along and tells you the truth of the whole matter, now we no longer have this teddy bear snuggled up to us, but now we have a raging tiger who wants to rip the offender to pieces.

Knowing now that this ego or tiger is only an illusion, but still finding it hard to truly realise this, I would have to recommend that we can at least play the game of taming this tiger or ego. So what we can do is gently talk to this tiger, let it know who the master is, keep a lead on it, when it gets out of hand be aware of this and pull back on the lead again, and again, just keep catching it out.

This will at least keep you in the Now, and less in the grip of the past and the imagined future. So here we are playing within the life story, but now we are becoming more aware of the story, and also that it is all just that, a story. So again you will start to be aware of your own story and also other peoples stories, this is where you will be as an actor on a stage. You will still be playing the game of being your name, raising your children, going to work to pay the bills but now you will start to realise that you are not the actor. You will realise that you are far more than just the actor, you are now the director, directing your life story, your life now falls into place, it will also have much more meaning to it, it really becomes a pleasure to live in this play now.

You are no longer needing things to happen in this play to make the once unconscious actor happy and content. You are now happy for the simple reason that you are, for the first time, really enjoying your life story. Also by you being more aware you will make those around you such as your family members, more aware and so it shall go on to one to the other, just passing the light on to the other.

We live in a world where we want more and more, each generation wanting more than the last generation. When we do get more we experience the pleasure for only a small time and then are off to seek the next pleasure—the whole problem is we now need a much bigger dose of pleasure to outweigh the last.

This vicious cycle we have got ourselves into is almost impossible to get out of. We have the suppliers continually feeding us more and more goodies to feed our addictions. We now know what's behind all this addiction, so at least now we are aware of its origin and its hungry appetite, so what are we going to do about it?

Well here I go again, we cannot do anything about it but to just see for what it is. We are no longer in the darkness, we have now shed light on the culprit and by doing so, we have now realised that it was this culprit that has caused all of our misery and suffering, and again the big joke is that its all an illusion, no, we don't like hearing that all the time do we?

Like here I am bursting this bubble that you have so dearly held close to you all your life, you have attached every single thing that you believe that makes you who you are. You have also made other bubbles out of other people, connecting them to your bubble and just like the bubbles on the head of a nice poured beer in a glass, these bubbles have made you drunk with desire, and as with the addiction of alcohol, you just can't get enough, so you are forever growing bubbles, or is that blowing bubbles?

Like I said earlier in the book it's fun to burst bubbles, so that's what I do, I'm a bubble burster. Those who have apparently Awakened to this whole circus, are for the one who is still asleep, a danger to be near, the Christ, the Buddha and all the rest of those that we have idolised, or shoved up onto a pedestal far from our reach are all dangerous to be near, to be near the one who is Awakened is like the darkness coming near to the light. It's like someone who continually tells everyone lies about their so-called life, and on top of all that, not realising that they are lies until they meet someone who finally tells them that what they are saying, is nothing but lies.

Now this is not going to be accepted by the raging ego, it's going to rebel like the furies tiger. It's going to call the one who has brought this message to their unconscious memory a devil, a mad man, a stick in the mud, and as I myself have been called many times, arrogant.

I have to agree that it does sound arrogant to the ego mind, the thing is when we come from this place from within we do sound as if we are speaking as an authority figure. The truth is this message is from the authority of our inner Being, or you could say it's a message from God. The scriptures that do have authority about them, that is a message to Awaken to our true SELF, the Christ if you like, are in fact from the writers own inner authority. This truth from within is intuitively brought to the surface through a mind that has been purified by the Awakening of the individual writer.

The ego mind is so scared of being found out, It has invested all of its energy to become what it is, but there is only One power and that is your true SELF, or if you like the power of One GOD. The whole thing is we must stop giving our power to this illusionary parasite, the ego.

Each cell in our bodies seem as if they are all working for their own good but when we look closer we realise that they are actually working as one in unity with the whole body. When these cells don't cooperate holistically with the body we then have what is called cancer or any number of diseases. All the healthy cells live and die for the good of the body, this is called apoptosis, but sometimes one cell might not die, this cell then produces more of these cells, to keep these cells alive they cause the body to produces its own blood supply, and then the whole growth starts to take over the body causing in the end the death of the body, and of course, itself. All nature works in harmony, everything working for the good the whole, I would say that the human race in its infancy also worked in harmony with nature, but because of our so called higher intellect we became too smart for our own good.

Of course we have made so called progress in our evolutionary journey, we have made ourselves much more comfortable but at what price? We are today caught in a world that we must work for the good of the economy, if we don't work hard to feed this economy we are looked at as being useless. If we don't go out to buy all the latest gadgets the economy is affected, then if we all run out and buy too much the economy is then also affected—the bankers are dictating to us all, adding all the time some stupid fee to cover some stupid made up story that seems to never be able to be understood by us ordinary folk.

But, just like sheep, we keep following the demands made on us by the greedy few who continually keep us under their thumbs. It certainly is a dog eat dog world, but unless we all do something about it we will always be the ones being eaten by these hungry dogs.

Behind all this is a big festering collective ego that we all have become part of and what to do with a festering ego? We need to squeeze the life out of it to get rid of the pus and the filth that has been feeding it. What has been feeding it? Greed, manipulation, and lies, we are controlled by the media, by the government, the banks and a million other things. This festering society that we are all part of, wants you and I to play its filthy game, but the catch is, we can never win, to the Awakened one this is all seen through.

Yes there is frustration, but this is felt in compassion for the sleeping who are caught within this trap, who are under the spell of these pigs who snort continually in our pockets taking everything they can. All this filth has become as a cancer to our natural way of living. We have forgotten our true connection to our mother nature, we have strayed away from our natural roots.

We don't need to give up all that we have but I believe that we need to at least put everything into perspective, we are becoming more comfortable bodily but we are also becoming more psychologically unhappy, mental illness such as depression and anxiety is becoming more prevalent, and this is actually happening in the so called richer and more so called advanced countries than anywhere in the world. Even though there are many so called poor people in the world as in third world countries, these seem to be happier over all, than the richer folk.

So as you can see collectively or individually, the ego has created much misery throughout our lives and all the time it was only an illusion of our own making.

Also now we are becoming more aware of not just our own ego and the ego of others, but also the collective ego of the whole of society. The more of us that become aware of what's happening, the more we will become happier and even further than this, the more of us who truly have disappeared into their true Being, and have returned to share their truth with others, the more we will become collectively Enlightened. Of course as I have already said, we are all pure Awareness already, but again we are all asleep in a dream of believing we are separate, and this is why we live in a world of greed and manipulation.

Most of us are trying to get what they can from each other, and not having any thought of what happens to the other, as long as we get what we want. We say that we love our own family more than any other but this is because they are just an extension of our own selves. When it comes to other families we don't think much about them, if they don't serve a purpose for our own need why bother? This is evident with the millions who are starving in this world, if they were of our own blood we wouldn't think twice to organise everything we can to help them.

We spend billions on the space race hoping one day to travel to other planets while our own is in starvation and poverty, we believe we are loving creatures but the truth is we are not, animals show far more love than we ever could, most animals live as a unity protecting each other family, not just their own.

We think we know what love is but we don't, as long as everything is going our way in the relationship we are happy but as soon as love dies we want out. The ones who don't want out try in vain to keep the relationship continuing, either because of insecurity of our own behalf, or because of the children, the children are then resented for keeping us in this toxic continuing relationship.

I feel that the human species once had an inbuilt psychic mechanism, which acted like an inner force that propelled us forward through our evolutionary journey, but as we became more of a thinking animal, where we could ponder on the past and the so called future, we began to compare ourselves to what we have and what we could have. We now realised that because of this future we needed something to make us happy for when we arrive there. We then observed that there are others who have obtained much compared to what we have, just like an animal that stores its food for the winter months so as to survive, we also started to save what we can but at the expense of other humans.

The feeling of pleasure is what is behind all evolution, it is what motivates us to move forward, if there is no pleasure, in say sex, why then bother? So here we are today with this inner mechanism to project us forward, now lost to the illusionary parasite, the ego. Of course we still have this inbuilt force to lead us forward but it is now being over shadowed by the illusionary ego. Instead of coming to the end of our evolutionary animal existence, and Realising now that we are at last living in heaven on earth, we have instead fallen asleep again in the garden of Eden, and again we are missing out on our pure Divinity, or inheritance from God.

So the Adam in the story of the old testament, did he ever Awaken or is he still asleep? I feel that he is still asleep but it doesn't have to be like this, we just need to realise our true nature, we need to realise that we have been asleep and now its time to Awaken.

So how did we fall into this deep sleep? Well as the story says that Adam ate of the tree of knowledge, of good and evil, this knowledge is what has put us all to sleep, we fell from our true nature to or false ego self. This false self became dualistic in its perception of what it thought life was, life no longer was lived in harmony with nature, we tried to be above nature, we believed that we were above the animals and even the earth itself.

We tried to beat it all into submission, so it would be under our powers to do with it what we wanted it to do. We then realised that nature had other plans for us so we started to beg her to obey our commands. We started to worship her so our crops would grow, but behind all this we were only pushed by greed, we only seem happy when things go our way, so when this God of nature obeyed our commands we were happy.

Because this God that we now have created seemed to be angry at times, with all the storms and drought that was wiping out our crops, we now started to project our unconscious hate of God by scarifying animals, even people, after all someone had to die, our revenge had to be satisfied somehow. Because we now were questioning everything around us and had no answers, we started to become superstitious of just about everything, in our once Oneness with nature, we had no need to question these things because they were not seen as separate from us, we were nature itself. I think it was Allen Watts that said, we didn't come into this world but we grew from this world, just as apples grow on an apple tree, so we grew also from the earth, the apple tree is Appling, the earth is peopling.

There is not one thing that makes us who we are that is not of the earth, the earth is also part of the solar system, the solar system is part of the galaxy, the galaxy is also part of the billions of other galaxies and so it goes on and on, and all this is ONE. When you look up at the stars as I love to do myself, just hold the thought that you are all that, you are that. Just feel that within you, within your whole Being, let yourself expand out towards all those stars out there and realise that there not really just out there, that there ONE with you, you just don't stop at the skin that is covering your body organism, you are One with all that there IS.

Unknowingly at the time, this is how I felt, all that there IS, I felt my whole body expanding outwards in all directions until I was One with all that there IS. In this what seemed to be a giant balloon, I felt that I had no boundaries, I felt that I didn't just stop at the edge of the enclosure of the skin that wraps and protects my body organism, I was all that there IS, but it was beyond just a bodily experience.

This is where words cannot convey to you beyond this boundary, this enclosure we call the mind body organism. So here we are after all this time a creature called a human being, the only thing that seems to be missing is the Realisation of its true identity, its true nature, something it lost many years ago.

31

The Human Race

I feel that we as the human race have been pushed too fast into a world that we are not quiet ready for as yet, even though we are more comfortable than ever, as a whole we seem to be becoming more unhappy and neurotic. We are like children that have been given everything they need and much more, because of this we are becoming more spoiled and as a result are expecting to have what everyone else has, and again much more also. Because of this way of thinking we now need mum and dad both working to pay the mortgage, and the two cars, that they are working hard to own. They also now have the greedy children who want more than any generation before them, and all this is labelled as progress?

Of course there's nothing wrong in having a world that is much more comfortable, but when we have an ego that just wants more and more on top of what we already have, this then is when we lose balance, we lose our sense of true identity and we are overtaken by this false greed caused by the ego getting out of hand, we have now become the slave of our own making. We have become so unhappy in this world that we need to stuff more and more into this inner emptiness, this feeling that we are lacking something.

This inner emptiness is caused by the ego keeping you clinging to the outside world, again we are out of balance. This inner emptiness is really calling to you to enter its silence, it knows that you have been unhappy, it wants the best for you, but because of the outside world that has you under its spell, you are feeling that this emptiness is against you, this outer balance has caused you confusion and this is what the ego wants, you are really your own worst enemy.

We are taught by society to believe that if we don't have all the latest toys or gadgets, that we are a nobody, if we don't own a computer or cellular phone then what good could we possibly be to a society, that needs you to participate in their game of greedily feeding the collective economy. This empty world that you feel within you is your resting place from the world of madness, this outer world is beautiful when the emptiness within is entered and realised from within, you must enter the outer from the inner for this is true balance, you cannot take the outer into the inner, your true treasures are stored only within.

This addiction for the outer world has completely put us out of balance and this is why we are not happy, or at least not for too much longer after we believe we have found what we want from the outer. After the fix that we have received from the outer, we continually need more and more fixes to satisfy our greedy needs and all the time not realising this. This emptiness is also felt when many retire from years of working, all of a sudden they are there with themselves, we don't really know ourselves—we have spent all our life knowing everyone else's life.

There is nothing wrong in having an interest in another's life but because of this we are again out of balance. This greed that we feed from comes in all sorts of ways that we probably would never realise, it can even be seen in those that we look up to, it could be someone who gives so much to a charity and wants everyone to know that they do this great work, all the time greed is behind their motive.

We have to be on guard also not to let this greed control our wanting to be more Aware, it will have us greedily trying to be aware when in fact we are completely unaware of what's happening, we can even become greedy for the silence within.

There are many books on meditation and every meditation is designed for you to get something or should I say at least most of them. The whole point of true meditation is to lose everything you have. You cannot store your treasures in heaven, heaven is already your treasure, but this is not enough for most—they want much more than mere silence, they want power, they want to be able to talk to angels, they even want to manifest whatever they want in their life and all because of their greed.

There are thousands of books out there that are offering you anything from contacting the spirit world to contacting fairies, this is all under the guise of spirituality. Religion may fade away further but this game of spirituality will eventually take its place with even more faith required to believe in it. Most of these games we call spirituality are only another way for the ego to disguise itself even further in the illusion, its all just another emotional smoke screen for this cunning ego to hide in.

There is only pure Being, anything else is Being expressing its SELF, all these spiritual mind games are just that, spiritual mind games. They only exist because of the mind, drop the mind and where are they, where are the sprits in this spirit world? Where are the fairies running around in the garden? They're nowhere to be found without the mind, in fact where are we without the mind? Without the senses we wouldn't exist. It's like when the tree falls in the forest if there are no hearing apparatus to hear sound, then how can there be the existence of sound. Yes there would be a vibration in Consciousness but it wouldn't be a sound that we would associate with the tree falling. And so is everything else just vibrations within Consciousness, even the book you are holding is a vibration, your fingers that are turning the pages is also a vibration, again we are all One in this pure soup of Consciousness, all vibrating at different frequencies, but still all ONE.

I do see these spiritual games as that, just games, we can be into Tarot cards or any other form of divination but its all there within Consciousness. Everything is connected, anything that is possible to pick up from divining is only within the Source, it has nothing to do with the cards, nothing to do with crystals, or crystal balls even. The so called Awakening is the disappearance into this Oneness of pure Being. It's you as the wave emerging back into the ocean, the many waves and formation above the ocean was only you, you were the same Source of this vast ocean. Many are clinging to the beautiful waves and formations, they are overwhelmed with the wonderful things that these waves brings to them, they're tasting the saltiness of the wave and formation and believing they have discovered the Ocean. We and everything else is part of the ocean, but to cling to just a single concept of this ocean is missing so much more, yes we will have concepts of how the saltiness of the ocean taste but that's all it will ever be, just a concept, just the finger pointing to the moon, not the moon.

32

Claim Your Inheritance

So you may be thinking right now why do I keep saying this is all so easy, it's who you are, when in fact it sounds as if this can never be obtained. Again this is why, because as I also keep saying it cannot be obtained, if you're trying to obtain this then you haven't really been listening to what I have been alluding you to.

When I speak to you from these words I am speaking to your higher SELF, I am trying to bypass the crap that you have collected throughout your life journey, if I speak directly to your mind body you will miss the whole point of what the words are pointing to. So right now I am letting you in on the secret, I feel now is the time to be more open about this so called Awakening, I'll be a little less obscure in my words.

The reason why I don't just come straight out and say it like it is, is because the ego will use it for its own benefit. So where do we begin? Well as you know now you are all that there IS, you are not the pimple you thought you were, you're not the illusionary ego that has attached itself to you like a parasite, you are none of these so stop acting like you are—come now and claim your inheritance.

You are the king of kings and lords of lords, take now your thorn on the right hand side of your Father, your Father in pure Consciousness or heaven if you like, you are his sons and daughters and you are all ONE as a family is ONE.

Now you have taken your claim, now you are in charge of your life. As a member of the human species, you came here to live this life, so you can see your marvellous works, the beautiful planets that you have created, the stars and all the other planets that go on and on forever.

Now you are remembering again that which you have forgotten, you have been in a dream that was brought about by your own doing, this was because you wanted to forget for a time who you truly were. You entered this dream so you would be as a child who could play in this dream that you made, discovering everything as new, as something you have never seen before, after all how could all this be a surprise if you already knew in advance. Yes this is why you wanted to forget who you truly are.

This dream you were in was a beautiful dream at first but somehow you were tempted to taste the fruits of good and evil, there have been many stories about your fall; these were written by those of you who were Awakened from their slumber. Over time these who have Awakened have been slowly trying to bring you back to your true nature, it is good to be as a child but its not good to stay as a child, for all children must grow into their fullness, and there also live the wonders of their lives.

In growing you were meant to mature spiritually and find your true Being once more. You have come a long way through billions of years of evolution, now its time again to take back your true identity. It's time for you to also help those who are still in their slumber, to help them to Awaken to their true nature, this may take time but time is nothing, it has taken billions of years to get to where you are NOW. In your true dwelling place this time concept means nothing. This message is for you who are now Awakened, go out now and tell all the world of your marvellous Self discovery, the SELF that includes all, for all are your brothers and sisters in Christ Consciousness.

But here's the catch, if you do go out and declare this to the sleeping world you will be trodden upon, you will be ridiculed for the sleeping world will not want you or anyone else disturbing their slumber. They are dreaming that they are the story, that they are the character of the story, but by you not playing alone as you should in their dream, you will be looked at as an arrogant disturbing jerk.

If you are Awakened to this lie you will not be disturbed by these words, but you will have compassion and deep understanding, because you were in the same boat once when you dreamt that you were the character in your dreaming. This dream world is the only world they know, it is taken extremely serious, so we need to tread softly and carefully, so as to not Awaken them to the lie that they are living under.

No one, while they are under the spell of the ego likes to be told that their whole life was just a lie, there is so much invested in this life of theirs, all their beautiful dreams, their hardships that they continue to feed on and tell anyone who will listen and give them a sympathetic ear. Of course there are times when we all need to share something to get it off our chest, but it's when we are stuck in the past continuing to live off this hurt and dragging it right through our miserable life that it becomes nothing but neurotic baggage.

We keep ourselves surrounded with as much drama as possible, we stick our noses in our grown children's affairs, we want everyone to remember our birthdays and want to be known as someone when we die. We never really know who we are, we only know what everyone else thinks about us, we also want everyone that we know to think they are what we think of them. With all this going on we never know who we are, we go to our graves living a life for everyone else and we miss out on ever knowing who we are, what a waste of a beautiful opportunity to enjoy your creations and to discover your true Being.

There are those who greedily believe that they will have many more lives to live and maybe one of them will be the one where they will Awaken, I'm sorry to say to these folk, that this is it.

Just as the Cosmos came into being and in the so called future will disappear back into Being, so do we as the mind body organism. We are compared to the Cosmos like a micro-universe, just as the Cosmos is born and expands out through space, so do we, we as the mind body organism becomes a micro-universe expanding outward until we also disappear back into pure Being. Every other mind body that is born is also a micro-universe unto themselves, there maybe millions of macro universes within and without our own that we don't know of.

We are so greedy that we come up with all sorts of ideologies to support our beliefs that we will continue on forever and ever. Just as the Cosmos that we know of will one day disappear back to where it came from, so we will also within our universe we call our life.

If we all knew this just imagine how we would live this life we have, we would enjoy each and every second, but sadly this knowledge in the wrong hands, would have those who want to get as much as they can from this once in a trillion year life. They would try to get everything they can from whoever they can, after all there's no hell so what have they to lose.

So fear keeps us on the straight and narrow it seems, while most of religion keeps us in fear of being sent to hell or everlasting damnation, many spiritual beliefs tell us that we must come back again and again until we have learnt our lesson.

This is all from the ego mind wanting to keep us under its illusionary demands, the ego doesn't want to die and it will formulate anything no matter what to keep itself alive, it doesn't know the truth so what it tells us is real to itself.

Just like the analogy I shared earlier, the light bulbs and believing they are separate, that they give their own light and each light is also separate but when the light bulb no longer can give its light, we then replace it with another light bulb. Now, no matter how many light bulbs we change there is never going to be a light bulb that is the same as the one before. It's the electricity that gives it light but the electricity never changes, its all the same electricity that is animating though all the bulbs. This is the same with us, each and every mind body organism is unique in its own way, this is because of genetics and programming, so when each and every mind body dies, so does the uniqueness die with it.

The pure being that animates through all the mind bodies is the same Source, this source is pure uncontaminated Consciousness. This Consciousness or Being, will also animate through all the other

mind bodies, that are born after the death of each mind body that are now departed.

There are so many belief systems out there that even after one has tasted their true Being, end up joining these beliefs. Spirituality has become as bad as religion with all its branches going in all directions. These people are only becoming trapped again by the ego that they believed they outsmarted, when in fact the ego has outsmarted them.

So here we are now with totally nothing, nothing to cling to, nothing to believe in, and all along you thought you were going to get something out of this book.

The thing is when we are without and totally nothing, we are actually in totally everything, when everything the mind thought it owned is gone there is left everything that the mind has never known. This pure Being, pure silence can never be known by the mind, the mind can label the experience one has when there is the disappearance into Oneness, but this is not what Oneness is. Again the Tao cannot be named. If you try and to name it, that is not what IS, when one or the apparent one experiences this Oneness, it does arise from within in a beautiful way, it is the most wonderful sensation that one could possibly have.

In fact most who have at least had a small taste of this Oneness, will try and try again to achieve this same beautiful inner feeling, just as one will again and again want to experience the pleasure of an orgasm. But it must be realised that no matter how beautiful this feeling is, no matter what beautiful poetry and emotion you add to it, that is never what IS. All this beautiful emotion and feelings are all secondary, they are only the shadow, yes a beautiful shadow but still just a shadow. There are many writings that are very beautiful to read, very poetic and inviting but again they are not what IS, they may open your heart to receive what IS, but they themselves are not what IS.

We must find the truth from within our own Being and of course our own Being is all One Being, its not a separate Being from someone else's Being, but this One Being is realised within our Self, from the recognition of remembrance that has been asleep for so long.

The game that we started has got out of control by the veil, that was erected between our true nature and our mind body conscious self, the mind body conscious unfortunately became overused by the thinking mind which the ego was formulated from. Because of the ego being formed we became more and more asleep until we fell into a deeper sleep like a coma.

As we all know sleep can be beautiful, we get greedy and want more after a full nights sleep, we lay there waiting again for the alarm to go off once more. So by understanding this you can easily see how all of this came about, how greed became so powerful, how we wanted what everyone else had at whatever price it was, even death and so we have wars.

You could write volumes on this, the many stupid wars that were fought throughout history, you could write volumes on how the belief systems of the world murdered millions upon millions of people, how the churches through greed believing that they alone had the truth, as if the truth can be held in one church or even by one person such as Jesus.

So by now you can see how hoodwinked we all have been but we don't have to be there any longer, do we? Yes it's truly time to Awaken from this nightmare. Just like any nightmare while we are in the dream it seems so real, and also can be very frightening but, when we Awaken we realise that it was only a dream, this is why I have been trying to lay the foundation before you, so as you will be ready for this Awakening. Like a map that is useful to identify the new territory that we are going to find ourselves, so is the foundation set before you, will help you when you do realise this whole nightmare was only a dream.

There are some that feel frightened of this Awakening, they're frightened that they are going to lose their identity, like someone who has had a hit on the head and is suffering from amnesia. There is no problem with this, you will still remember everything about who you are, but now you will be Awakened to the reality that it was all a story. Of course we still have to play within the story, we still have our family to provide for, we still have our jobs to attend to, the point is now we are playing the game but now we realise that, that's what it is, a game.

If the ego is still there then there will be resentment of knowing that its only a game, that will not do for the ego, it has too much invested in this game. To be a game for the ego is knowing that its been found out and with this the ego knows that it will only be time before it will die. When one realises that it's only a game, then they will over time give up the hold that the ego had for so long, its like when we grow from a child to an adult, no matter how much we pretend to play childish games, we still know that we are adults, and even feel embarrassed when it is pointed out by someone who is mature, as we should be also. So now the game is seen for what it is, just a game, and the actor now realises that that's all he was all a long, just an actor.

Now that you know the truth of your mistaken identity, what are you going to do about it? Also now that you know that you can't do anything about it, then what to do?

The only thing you can do is just give up, give up the search, give up the path, also give up all that has brought you this far. When you come to this stage of just giving in to what IS, its so beautiful to rest in the arms of Being, or God if you like using that pointer, it doesn't really matter. In this rest of silence we can feel the heartbeat of God, just feel it beautifully pulsating within, if you can't don't worry just concentrate on your own heartbeat and imagine that it is becoming in tune to the Cosmic note of the universe. Just like a tuning fork that is struck and sounds a note that resonates with any other object, that also holds that note pattern within it, there is a background silence that permeates through all that there is, this silence is sometimes known as the OM—the pure sound of the universe.

This is not to be taken literally as we do with making the sound as we meditate, but still this can also be beneficial in bringing us to the pure Essence of the silence within. You can use the OM sound or you can feel the rhythm of Being from within, aligning your rhythm with the universes heartbeat if you like, it doesn't really matter.

Try not to cling to any technique as the technique is only a tool to bring you there. When you are there, when you feel deep within that you are part of all that there IS, then just let go, feel yourself fall like falling from an aeroplane, but in this case you have no parachute, this is where some become frightened, but don't worry you cannot be hurt, just go with the fall. If you have tried this far and nothing happened, don't worry about that, it's not a race, but keep remembering that you are already there, you're just trying to remember it. Die daily to the mind body and be renewed in Consciousness, each day is your chance to be where you are, here, NOW, you haven't gone anywhere, its just your mind that takes you to where it wants you to be.

Of course we need to remember things that happened in the so called past, to recall something that is needed in the present, this is using the memory of yesterday for today, or the eternal NOW. Any fear that you may have is also from the past, if you had no memory of what is dangerous you wouldn't survive, so memory is important for us but it's when the past takes over our being here, NOW, in the eternal present, that it becomes suffering in the present.

You cannot really try to be in the present of NOW, because that's where you are, always. Just as you are always pure Being, or Enlightened—it's just the same story over and over. This is why I am repeating myself over and over in this book, what could I possibly add that really hasn't already been said by those before me. There is only One Truth, but there are many ways to describe this Truth, depending on all sorts of reasons, such as language, culture, the times of which it is shared, but the thing is its all the same Truth. Unfortunately there has been a lot of meddling with this beautiful Truth that many in the past have shared, leaving us today with half baked truths, and again all this truth that I have just spoken of is not the actual truth, again they are all pointers, pointing to what IS.

33

We Are One

This Enlightenment that so many are trying to achieve is looked at as something that only a selected few can ever reach, this is not true because there has never been a single person Enlightened, even Jesus was said to say, "that of myself I can do nothing but the father does all the works", so if there is Enlightenment then it's not of ourselves but from Consciousness, its SELF, that animates through us all.

This inner flow is continually there but the only reason that we are not conscious of it is because of the mind body organism. It needs to be to a degree this way, so as we can be the creature we are meant to be, but because through evolution, we have now come to a stage where we are becoming too smart for our own good, or is that too dumb for our own good.

We have missed out on the beauty of inner Self Awareness, that should have been part of our evolvement. We would have been living in a world of peace and pure happiness, we may have not been so called advanced as we are, but still we would have been contented with whatever we would have had.

We have got ourselves in a situation where we are not happy, even with all that we do have now, it seems the more we have in this world the more we want, because of this we need more and more people to buy it all. We are taking more and more from mother earth, we have become as a parasite on the face of the earth, and one day she is going to scratch us all off, in fact she does this already, in ways such as earthquakes and other so called natural disasters. But with all that said, here we are anyway, I do feel that we will further evolve to a higher collective Consciousness but why wait? We at least can help to lift mankind up by just being more Awake, and by just a few being more Aware is all that is needed to start us onto a new adventure towards collective Enlightenment.

This will be truly when the second coming of Christ will return and rain upon the face of the earth. We are all born in Christ, we then forgot who we are, this is the Christ born within, the world and all its illusions have made us all forget this, but when we remember all this again, then this will be the returning of the Christ.

When we get the idea that there was only one Christ, for all time, out of our heads, and realise that this Christ is our very nature, that the Christ is our mediator within that communes with the father who is our true Being, who we are all ONE in. Then it's time to take your true identity and stop living under the guise of an illusion, its time to stop believing you are a sinner and realise that you, that is your true inner Being, can never sin, when you don't realise this, then you are by the sin, as in the new testament Greek word, meaning "off target". Also as I said before if your target is God, or your inner Being, then you cannot miss, it's just too big of a target.

So now lets meet our true Self Identity, so I'll introduce you to you by way of introducing you to me, after all you and I are ONE. So my name is Oneness and I AM all that there IS, so I Am glad to meet you, even though I have always Known you, I have been in this world from the time this world came into Being, this world has never really gone anywhere, it has only gone through one change after the other, One Cosmos to the next and in micro form one human being to the next, all in their own way a new universe been reborn, but each being unique in their own way.

So hello to you . . . I can see that you have a uniqueness of your very own but more than that I can see that you are as I AM, isn't that wonderful, here I AM talking to my SELF, can you see that? Can you see that you are looking in a mirror and it is I that is looking at you looking at me and we are ONE. So now you have become as I, can you feel that, can you feel that you and I are ONE, these words that you are reading are the echo of your own Being, can you hear that?

So now we have meet at last, you have been waiting for this very moment all your life, and it is NOW here. Just disappear into it, into this moment of NOW, imagine I am taking your hand and leading you within your true Being, just let go of what's pulling you away from I. Don't cling to these words that you are reading, see beyond the words, see beyond the image that you have, of I holding your hand, just keep coming within to me, just keep going with your inner Being that is holding your hand, gently bringing you further and further inwards. Don't be frightened for it is only I, you and I are ONE, you and I are pure LOVE.

Feel that LOVE as you come closer and closer to your true Being, don't worry I am still holding your hand, now look down at my hand and you will see that it is your hand, you yourself is holding, for we are ONE. There is no other, you and I have always been ONE, can you remember? Is it all coming back to you, can you remember when we were children, when we use to play together, I was the one that you used to imagine was your friend, but then you grew and gave up your childish ways, but in this giving up you also gave me who is you, away. You then forgot all about me but I was with you all the time, yes I was there in your so called bad times and your so called good times, you always had a feeling that I was there didn't you? And you were right I was always there. So here I am again, yes it's me your imaginary friend but now I am here not as an imaginary friend, but as your own SELF, what more of a friend could you ever have?

It was I who was you, who you once talked to, it was also I who was you who you longed for, the search was always for I who is you but you didn't realise that did you? So here we are again, meeting each other through the words of this book you are holding, and reading from, it's a small world isn't it? Everywhere you go you are there with me who is you, even if you never remember me I will still be there within you, if you die not ever knowing me it really doesn't matter, because in the end I will be there to greet you and then you will remember me who is you, you and I have never parted, we are

ONE, everyone who is reading these words is also you, and I, and altogether we are ONE.

Here we are having this dialogue when all this time there was only you, you thought you were talking to I, but all the time you were talking to your SELF, you see there is only you, your SELF. Now forget about I who was talking to you and realise that it was you all along. This is your book, you wrote the words in this book, you have written all the words of every beautiful spiritual inspiration that you have ever read. There is only one truth and that is who you are, and all the time you thought you were separate from the words, you thought you have to learn from the words but the words can't teach you anything, because you are already That which the words are pointing to, you only need to remember.

Most times when we try to remember something that just won't come, we cannot seem to bring it to mind no matter how we try, then all of a sudden when were not even thinking about it, it just pops up from nowhere, it was always there in our memory. This is similar to our remembrance of our true nature, it's always been there within our whole Being, in the background of everything we do. It's like the silence of the screen which our whole life is projected upon, just for a moment stop the projecting and just be with the screen, this screen is our pure Being, its our true home. This is where I am leading you to, this is where you will remember again who you truly are, you have been lost out there in the world that you thought was real, in a world you never really could fit into. This is why you were lead to this moment, this is why you were lead to read this book, so here you are just about to find this beautiful Love that you thought you lost a long time ago.

Do you remember all the hurt you have experienced throughout your life? Do you remember the times you felt so alone, even when you were with others around you? There was always something there that you could never quite put your hands on, something that you could never touch, you felt this inner longing to be home but you never knew where your home was to be found. Well here I am still leading you within to your true Being, are you going to enter with me?

Now its time for you to let go and fall into the pure silence that you have now at least felt, that's it just let go, now spend the next few minutes going within, feel my hand holding your hand which is really your hand, we are ONE. Now feel this silence, just feel it right through your whole Being for this is where we are going to fall into, when you are ready come back to feeling my hand holding your hand which is really your hand for we are ONE.

As I speak these words feel them within, not just on the pages that you are reading from, for these pages are not what you are entering into, they are only pointers that I am using to guide you, so now forget about everything out there and enter with me NOW. That's it, just let go, don't worry for I am still here with you, I have always been here with you, now close your eyes and feel the beautiful silence within, feel the beautiful Love that you have never felt before, just feel it.

Now I am going to let your hand go, the hand that is really your own hand as we are ONE. So I am letting go of your hand, and now you are for the first time, for so long now, finally free, just feel that freedom of being light, oh, so light, no clinging to anything, just pure freedom. Now just stay in that freedom, get to know it all over again, yes in this freedom you will start to remember that it was always there with you, it was there and gone, but still you are remembering it all again. You won't remember this freedom in your mind for that is where you forgot this pure freedom, you will remember it through your whole Being, so just let this freedom be there, for ever how long it needs to be. I can only leave you there, where you are NOW, I cannot do any more for you, in fact it was you who has brought you to this freedom, for we are ONE, now that you have realised this, all you have to do now is take back your individuality, individual ONENESS.

Now, if nothing happens within these words to you, well it's no big deal. Don't forget that you are already that, its just the remembrance of that, that you will experience, just keep coming back to these few pages and let me again take your hand and again we will go within together. You just need to give yourself time, to again become familiar with your SELF, just imagine meeting your twin that you never knew you had, Wow, wouldn't that be something. And here you are in this process of meeting your true Being, meeting the very you that created this whole universe, the very you that can never be born and can never die. I must say also if there has been this connection and you have disappeared into this pure Essence, believe me you will know, you will feel brand new, you will start to feel everything as if for the very first time.

To you, who are remembering now, I would say stop trying to go any further, you have fallen into this pureness, not by trying as you believe you did, but by just letting go of all that has been holding you back. The words never did anything for you, it was what was between the words, it's what you subconsciously recognised as truth to you, it just happened by its own accord, to you I say welcome to YOU, your true SELF.

Now back to you who still believes you haven't arrived, don't feel that you have missed out on something, the truth is that those who apparently have Awakened are you also, again we are all ONE, there is no one who is in this world that has something that you don't have. Jesus, the Buddha and all the rest that we seem to idolise, also have nothing that you haven't got. There is no place for jealousy or envy in this knowing or remembrance of your true Being, there is no one you could possibly envy because to do so is ignorance of who you are. I have nothing that you haven't got, and what I am sharing in this book is to remind you of this truth, that you may remember again.

The thing with belief systems that tell us that such and such has achieved Enlightenment, is that they keep the truth away from us, we focus all our energies on the one that has been lifted up by others. We then put ourselves below them and we are continually told that we can never be where they are. It's time now to kick the pedestal from under them and look them right in the eyes, that have so long looked down on you, then you can say with all truth, that you are where they are, that you have always been there. But do not do this from the mind, this will only be the ego envying, what it so desires to have for its greedy self, you know now that you are not the mind body or the ego, so there is no need to even consider being anything else, you are It.

I keep repeating this to you over and over for the reason that you may easily slip back to the illusionary self, believe me its waiting anxiously there for you, it maybe just an illusion but it has great power over you, it can only have this power if you let it take it away from you. So again take my hand that we may always be together as ONE, when you are ready then let go of my hand, which is really your hand as we are ONE. Now keep repeating what I have shared with you, if you are not there yet, you will be very soon, and remember again your already there, you only need to remember this, that is all.

34

So What Now?

So what happens after this apparent Awakening? How do you carry on in the world now? Well the same as you always have, but now you are Awake and you can see what's being going on all around you, all the time while you were asleep. You will slowly start to shed your old self and your old ways at looking at the world, you are like a caterpillar who has been asleep in his cocoon and now he is slowly emerging from the cocoon. The caterpillar that has turned into the butterfly must emerge from his cocoon slowly, if you force the butterfly with its delicate wings you will damage them and he will not be able to fly. You are now the same, you must slowly emerge from your cocoon made from all your precious programming and conditioning, slowly you will become familiarised with the life you were meant to live.

The ego at this time will be stirred up and there will be much dust, which is the fragmenting programming and conditioning being broken up, it will not just magically disappear but will linger for quite awhile, but now you know, when I say that you know I mean really Know.

Before this inner knowing your knowing was of the mind, you read about it earlier in the book or any other book, and all you really had was an intellectual understanding, now you have been within and truly experienced this Knowing or Truth for your SELF. When this inner Knowing has been reached and the penny has dropped, you may feel so happy that you just start laughing, or even crying, but the tears will be of pure inner happiness. For the first time you will experience a happiness that you just can't explain.

We can label this happiness with past conditioning and use words to try to describe it, I felt this as if being home at last, or as being One with all that there IS. It really doesn't matter what you want to call it, but just don't forget whatever we call it, that isn't what IS. You will find that you will want to run out and tell all the world, but be prepared for a world that just doesn't want to know, or a world that will only believe you are crazy, don't be disheartened by this because this is only showing you that you have truly Awakened.

If you run out and tell the world with something that they all understand, believe me you haven't really found anything, again the mind cannot understand all this, its beyond the mind as you have discovered for your SELF. But that being said, yes we have to start from somewhere, and of course that would be with using pointers but at the same time not offering anything, for as you know now, what could you offer that they already haven't got. All those who are asleep, even the ones who are searching for this so called truth, can only be where they are, as long as they are caught in the story of trying to find the path that will take them away from the story, that's where they will stay, in the story of trying to get out of the story.

There are those also who believe in their story, that they have found this thing called Enlightenment and will also show the signs of one who has disappeared into Oneness, but these same people will still believe that there is much more to be done, that they need to be more Awakened, this too is just another trap erected by the illusionary ego.

The thing is with this so called Enlightenment its really no big deal, why would it be when in fact it's just who you are, there are so many who take this search for this elusive dream so serious, they believe that there is going to be this big event of fireworks or some big orgasmic climax. Because of this invested hardship of trying to get to this so called place of Enlightenment, this is the very thing that will keep you from ever disappearing into pure Oneness, this is why if you have been searching hard to be where you are all ready, you should just stop and rest in your inner Being.

You will never find this outside of your self, you will never find this outside in books, lectures or weekend workshops. These may bring you to the realisation that you cannot do anything and in this case that's all they can do, the same as this book you are reading, as I have already said it's not in the pages, if anything it's between the words and not even that.

So there is no need to save all your money and go off to India to find yourself, unless of course you want to go to India not expecting anything to happen—in this not expecting the unexpected may be revealed to you, the remembrance brought back to you. In this Realisation of what IS you come to a standstill, but where you are standing Now is always holy ground. You have now declared the Father from within, you are Now reflecting God and all His glory, you and the Father are Now One.

There are all sorts of beautiful scriptures and language that we can use to describe the indescribable, there's beautiful poetry also and all these can pull the heart strings which then emotion arises. What we need to know is that the emotion that arises is in most cases, is emotion that is stirred up from past memory, many are so attached to their beliefs and ideologies and within these beliefs they have projected their whole life story, especially the emotional side of the story. For example the Father and the Son of God are unconsciously seen or felt, as their own parents, or even in their relationships, its this pulling towards its Self that we feel the emotion, and where we get confused.

This false love is projected on to just about anything you can think of, we project this love on such things as Jesus and we believe that this Jesus loves us no matter what, but what can you say about such a thing, after all how could an imaginary figure do any wrong to you, how could your teddy bear ever hurt you or do you wrong? Such words as these to the sleeping multitude would be taken personally, they would believe to say such words is being heartless and cruel, to their treasured beliefs they hold so dearly. For this reason we must question the motives behind our idea of what we believe to be love, there is no danger in doing this, you're not going to lose anything but you will gain all by doing so, after all you are pure Love its SELF.

The trouble with all these past emotions is that they steal from us the NOW, they poison the energy that is coming from within. This inner energy is pure love, pure life force, but because it comes from within it must also come through the contaminated mind, until the mind is made to be at rest and silence prevails we will only bring to the surface a shadow of what's really there. All these words that I use to try to share this inner being, such as love, Consciousness, Being, God, are all the same, there all from the same Source.

So now we have thrown away all our accumulated beliefs, all our ideas of what we always thought love was. We are now standing here on holy ground, no need to take off your shoes as Moses did, when his God appeared to him in a flame burning in a small bush, you now know that you are not the mind body organism, so why take off your shoes? The man Moses in the old testament story was ignorant of his true identity, but you are not now, you have more inner knowledge than any Moses could ever have. Moses also built an outer sanctuary to make sacrifices to his God, killing innocent animals for their God so he would forgive their sins, all that they tried to do to satisfied their God was all from the outside world. This is what so many are still doing today, trying to find favour with an outer God, this is also why there has been so many wars in the name of this outer beast, this is what true sin is, to believe that your true Being is out there somewhere while your true target is within.

The outer objective world is so muchpart of the senses, that we are so captivated by it, but because we are sentient beings we do need this to a degree, but its when we are lost in the illusion of believing it's the only reality, that we suffer. Of course the outer world is here, it's what we believe we live in but this world that we see and touch is here and gone, its not permanent, it's like the wave upon the ocean—it's here and gone—it was never the reality of what it really was, the Ocean.

We must not get caught up in the outer or even the inner world, we only use the inner world as a pointer only, in the ultimate reality there is no division at all. So we need not get caught up in the outer or inner so called worlds, just forget the pointer for now they have served their purpose, just be in the silence, and forget everything that I have told you this far. Even if there has been a disappearance, you will find that the mind will still be there trying to philosophy all that has brought you to your SELF. You will try to work out how you got to where you are, you will try to work out a plan so as to show others, this is the ego trying to take claim of your Truth that can never be put into words, but don't worry this is bound to happen.

As I have said earlier after the disappearance, I myself wanted to tell the world, I also tried to make some formula using what I discovered and also other pointers that I have read about, and again no one wanted to listen. There is nothing wrong with telling the world but we have to make sure that what we say is not of the ego wanting to be in the spotlight, wanting to have disciples, wanting to put on workshops, wanting everyone to come to him. We already have plenty of these to keep us entertained, yes they do have their good points but they will never be able to tell others that they don't need to be here with them.

They will want you to go on a long journey with them, they will have you doing all sorts rituals, even standing on your head. No, fi rst get to know your SELF, your true Being, you already have been introduced and you have meet who you truly are, there is no more to do but be still and know that you are GOD, not the false God you thought you were but the true being of Consciousness.

35

Suffering

Another thing I must bring up here is suffering, as long as we believe we are suffering we can never be whole, we must find the one who is suffering and why they are suffering. I remember when I was shot along the highway all those years ago, I would keep that story playing over and over in my mind—of course it wasn't something that happens normally in someone's life and it was a very frightening experience—but still I continued to replay this story over and over again. The thing was that I didn't realise that I was so over taken by this event, I even found myself wanting everyone to know about my story, I felt as if I was a soldier who had returned home wounded and ready to be recognised for his bravery. I would tell the listener of my tragic story all the fine details, I would tell them the calibre size of the bullet, the big 303. I would play the story over and over again in my dreams and would often awaken from nightmares of being cornered in a house with the gunman. I felt as if I was a victim of the world, at least I had an interesting life to talk about, and even though this life was tragic at least it was a life.

With the many other tragic stories of my life that were being added to the existing one, my life seem to be full of pain, pain that I was becoming addicted to, at least subconsciously. In the disappearance into pure Being, I realised that I wasn't this mind body and all of its tragedy it has accumulated and filed away. The story of being shot, raped, nearly murdered more than twice, . . . it wasn't me and had nothing to do with me. Of course the pain of being shot and the cancer that I went through was there and yes it was very painful but now I didn't own it, I was now the observer watching.

This ignorance of not realising that you are not the body is the cause of all suffering, like I said the body itself will feel pain, that's what its designed to do, but its when we own the pain and add it to our story, and feel that we need to keep the story forever in our memory to be brought up when we need our next fix. This pain that we keep bottled up can sometimes get so overwhelming that it can actually bring us out of suffering, this is when we come to a point where we just completely give in to the suffering.

When giving in we drop the story and everything to do with the story. We become so used to living in this pain body that we really don't know any better, we don't realise what is on the other side of the mountain. When this pain is given into we are left with who we are, now who we are can be lived, can be free, it's not that we allowed anything to enter us, its just that we have let go of that which was hiding what was already there.

We must realise that we are the cause of our own suffering, no one else can give it to us, others can hurt the body, even kill the body but they cannot cause our suffering.

When I was shot yes I was in pain for a long time, the body had to recover from the gunshot wound but whatever I carried from there was my own suffering, the memory of the story of being shot—I carried this like a roll of film and continued to watch it over and over again. As long as we continue to unconsciously carry the ego, we will always be living our life through suffering, without the ego taking first place in our lives there cannot be any suffering, for there is now no one to take ownership and continue to deliver us our addictive fix.

We see this suffering all around us, especially through the media, of course there are horrible things that do happen around the world but the media wants to rub it right into our face, it wants us to be overcome by their story, it wants us to feel as we ourselves are in the story, it wants us to believe we live in a world that is dangerous

and fearful. Keeping us all in this state of mind keeps us alert and continuing everyday to watch their news for more and more disasters, this also keeps the society huddled together believing we all need each other. Of course there are times we do need to be with each other but not because we need to, not because we are afraid but because we are like one big family, sharing what we all have to make a better world, not a fearful world.

So you may ask, why does this so called God allow all this suffering? Well as long as you see yourself separate from the world, you will always see suffering all around you, don't forget you are the world, you are not separate from it, in reality you should ask yourself that question, after all you your SELF, created this world and everything in it. A good way at looking at suffering is to see it as creativity, something that has appeared before you, something that is there for you to learn from. If we put our hand in the fire it burns, the body is trying to tell you something—not to put your hand in the fire. If suffering arises its telling us not to be there in the suffering, not that we should forever run from it but to be conscious of this suffering, so as not to repeat it, and not carry it with us throughout our lives.

Would we carry the fire that burnt our hand with us? So when suffering arises see for what it is and deal with it, then drop it, it has served its purpose, it is no longer needed. Many believe that pleasure is happiness when all along it's only the opposite of pain, both are from the mind, both are from the senses that are registered in the brain and then are projected through the mind. True happiness is who you are, it's there within you for no reason, it doesn't need a reason to be there. When this inner happiness is felt and projected through the mind, yes it does seem to be pleasure, but unlike pleasure it is there for no reason, whereas pleasure is sought after.

When you look out and see the stars at night and a feeling of inner happiness arises, you never went outside to seek the happiness, but it just bubbled up for the simple reason that you feel within that your home is out there. When you live in this inner happiness you will see your home everywhere, outside and inside of your whole being, in fact you will feel there is no outside and inside, you will see the Oneness that you truly are without boundaries. If the objective world is being transient and only perceived by the senses, then all suffering which is out there is also perceived by the senses, therefore only an illusion.

When this is understood not intellectually but from our true being or our inner Knowing, the illusion of suffering and good and bad are now discovered to be not there at all. With this inner knowing we live our life in harmony with what we call the natural world or nature, the outside world maybe still transient but now we are at least, without suffering, why waste your creation of making you and the world out there just to live in an imaginary hell?

36

You Can Not Do Anything

For those who are still banging their heads against the wall over all this, who are fighting against the ego, all I can say really, is to read again the former pages, the ego will not let you see the signs that point to what IS, it will keep the words to the surface and not let them stimulate the inquiring inner Self. So here I will repeat again what I have shared earlier, just so it will be absorbed more in the depths of your soul. If you are still fighting remember that you cannot do anything, your fighting will only strengthen the illusionary ego, as I have said over and over you must do nothing but surrender, just let go of trying to do anything. To live in this world ignorant and asleep, is much better than going through your whole life fighting for something that you will never achieve.

As I have said also you are already That, but then you might say, "But I don't feel like I'm that," the trouble here is that you are after something, a reward, a Cosmic climax, instant happiness. Yes these things can happen but there not what IS, there only the shadow of what IS.

This disappearance into Consciousness for my apparent life, was of great joy but a joy that I have never felt before, there was no reason for it, it was just there, I just laughed and laughed but I didn't not know why at first. Now this doesn't mean this is how it should be for you or anyone else, for someone else it maybe just be, ohh, I see . . . and that's it.

Its like when you go somewhere, say on a holiday, you have all these expectations of how its going to be, you've read all the colourful brochures, you read all about the people but you really have no idea until you arrive there. When you do arrive you may be more excited than what you thought you were going to be, or again you might be let down by not having your expectations meet. This is the same with this so called Enlightenment, you've probably read many books on what others have said about their own experience. To the ego that is still there, it all sounds so wonderful that it wants the whole thing for itself. So now we have greed, so behind our innocence of wanting to disappear into Consciousness, all the time it was just greed and because of this unconscious greed we can never totally disappear.

There is no right way or wrong way to disappear, there is no written law and even if there were it doesn't mean anything, it's just another trick by the ego, there are those who have found this through meditation, but that doesn't mean you, yourself, will find it through meditation.

Mediation isn't the answer, its still the question, until you disappear in meditation or any other way, or no way, it doesn't matter, its not found in any way, it just apparently happens it that way.

I didn't even know what this word Enlightenment really meant or what it pointed to, I was never consciously after it, even though I have read books on Eastern Philosophy it never occurred to me what it was really all about, it just all sounded nice to me, ... maybe the deeper side of me was stimulated?

I think the reason why we hear more of these cases of apparent Enlightenment, where the person has really been down to hell, where they have been so overcome by the suffering mind, where they have just thrown in the towel, it wasn't because of the suffering but because of the letting go of everything and resting in the arms of the Father, or pure Being.

I remember the time that I cried out to whatever was out there, I cried like a little boy who had lost his mummy, and in one way I had, I lost my true Identity with the Realisation that I was with God all along. He or She was my very heart and everything that I was, was from Her.

This is why we seem to have this longing to be home again, we feel deep within that we don't really belong here. This is felt because we are thinking in duality, we still haven't realised that we never really left our home at all. But still, this longing is bringing us closer at least to what we believe we have lost, it's really when we have disappeared into our SELF that we remember all, that is, in the inner Knowing that cannot be conceptualised.

There are some who say that they are usually happy and feel as if they should be more sad and depressed, so as to enter this Awakening. I feel that in this case they haven't found true happiness at all, and the feeling of missing something that they feel they should have, is the stirring of inner Being calling them home. Or should I say, helping them to Realise that they are already home. It's like the ocean calling the rivers to enter back into it, when this Realisation is entered we then Realise that we are the rivers and the ocean.

So we may read all sorts of stories of how one disappeared and reappeared to tell their story, but that's all they are, stories. I have told you my story and my story was what was revealed through my particular mind body organism, your story will be what was revealed through your own mind body organism. The mind is only our tool but because it has been through so many years of contamination, it can never really be pure, in the sense of letting pure consciousness through. Even if it could, pure Consciousness or Being has no agenda or thought of its own, it's just pure silence.

I myself like reading what others have to say about their own apparent experience of Consciousness. Some are just ordinary everyday experiences, nothing spectacular just a simple Awareness, then you get others who say they have experienced a beautiful Utopia climax and again I have to say that its not the experience that is pure Being, the experience is again the after thought, the expression that comes through the mind. You see there are so many claiming that they have found this Enlightenment and they then try to sell it to others, they dress it all up and make it sound so inviting. It's like they are hanging a carrot in front of a donkey, the donkey then chases the carrot but can never reach it. This is the reason that I cannot really offer you anything that you don't already have, I don't want to hang a carrot out in front of you. I have given you some things to play with but I have never told you that these will bring you to your true Being. I have given them to you because while you are still believing you are the mind body this is what you will want to work with. So by the many other things here I have shared, maybe if you are under grace, you may reach your inner Being and maybe there will be a remembrance of your true nature, your true Identity, but I cannot guarantee you Enlightenment—how can I when that is who you really are, that is your true Being.

37

The Dog is Fed

As long as there is the belief that you are the mind body, then you will need a technique. I know I have said over and over that there is nothing you can do, but this really means nothing to those who are still under the illusion, but I have to lay the foundation for you first. The structure that you are building may need to be torn down over and over, but the foundation will always be there to keep you balanced.

The deeper you go into your true Being the less effort you will keep putting into it, when you have arrived, all effort will naturally drop away and you will be in pure Bliss. Effort, paths, beliefs, ideologies will all disappear from your grasp and you will be free.

There are those who have come to this Bliss and have tasted of its freedom, who have also wanted more and more, they cannot let go of the beautiful story of being on the path that they have created. There maybe a group that they meet with and just can't imagine not going there religiously, to discuss with each other their path and how they are making progress. They are more interested in the the label, "mystery", than the actual Realisation in the mystery.

To some this inner discovery seems too boring, there isn't enough to stimulate the ego mind, these seem to only have a foot in the door, but cannot let go of what they are holding onto, outside to enter in. So there are those who believe that they are Awakened, and still feel that they need to discover more to be even more Awakened. There is either Awakening or there is not, this idea of continuing the journey is still the crafty ego trying its hardest to keep you back from ever Knowing your true SELF.

When one has apparently Awakened there will be no more wanting to get somewhere where one isn't already, yes there will still be residue of the ego but now its seen for what it is, when it arises you just see it and laugh at it, or whatever your expression is when you see something that is not really there. There will be times also when you may get pulled down stairs by the illusionary ego, and maybe for a short while forget that you came downstairs, then there's the remembrance—Ha Ha I caught you!—and there's no big deal, all you do now is go back upstairs, the dogs been feed and everything is in order. Just like a good pet owner you show the illusionary dog who's boss, when you have come downstairs and have taken the dog out for a walk, you keep it on a lead. I have found this myself as I spend most time alone at home which I love to do, but when there's the occasion to mix with others who don't understand you, you can if the dog happens to get off the lead, get caught up in the neurotic stories of others. Of course we must also have compassion and understanding for the sleeping world, for we were there also once, and we can still be dragged back on occasion, so its not feeling that one is better, its just now one is Awakened to what is going on.

To the still sleeping they will see this as being arrogant, which I have been accused before on occasion, I had to learn how to apply myself and guard my words so as not to sound arrogant. Others, such as Jesus was looked upon as being arrogant also, what he said was what the sleeping people of that time didn't want to hear, they wanted to stay in their outer ritualistic religious ways. They couldn't believe what he said, they thought that he was saying that he, Jesus, was God, but because they believed in a separate God, Jesus sounded as if he was blaspheming.

Recently I was on a spiritual forum which I thought I would check out, I could see there were some who were after this blissfulness or inner Realisation. So I thought that I would share my story of what I apparently experienced, but I found out that there were many who didn't what to listen to what I had to say, they even attacked me for the things I said, of course there wasn't anyone to attack, but I have to admit I found myself saddened by this. It wasn't that I wanted them to listen, and do what I wanted them to do, it was just that I could feel their frustration and just wanted to give reassurance that they are there already. I was accused of being arrogant and a know all, and all I was doing was letting them know that there is nothing hard about all this and again to remind them, they are there already.

The thing is, again most don't really want the Awakening, this is because the ego is so strong and for you to realise this means death of the ego. By saying that you are already there is just too simple for the mind, the mind has heard from those who believe that they are Awakened, how you must come to them for a weekend or join their congregation, so you can learn how to achieve this, because they believe they have found the way to do it. Of course there are those who have great teachings, and people do go to them, but if there is an Awakening, its not because of the so called Guru, Awakened or not, it just apparently happened that way.

I just live my life as if nothing spectacular had happened, I did at the time of the apparent Awakening feel like I was ONE with all there is, and it was very beautiful, the laughing episode, the love that swirled within my whole Being, but I don't try to hold onto this experience, the so called experience was all that was needed. Like the analogy of the holiday where we have expectations and when we do finally get there it's nothing really like how we thought, either being overwhelmed or disappointed.

Again many do have expectations after Enlightenment, if there is a genuine Awakening, then the experience is felt through the mind body but because the one who has been Awakened has realised that all is ONE, they simply need no more convincing, they have seen the light, there is no more to be seen. After the realisation one simply goes back to what they have always loved doing. If you carry on trying to find this Awareness all over again, just to feel the feeling that came with it, then you haven't really found anything. It was just your mind again playing tricks, pretending it's Awake.

This is where the false teachers emerge from thinking they are Enlightened, they are very dedicated to their teachings and can actually be of some good, just as any teaching can be, but the problem is they will still have you trying to find something that they themselves have found. Because they have never really disappeared into Being they will be more like the holiday brochure, offering you something that they themselves have never seen.

Even if you go to a teacher that has disappeared into their Being, he or she still cannot offer you anything, again because they have nothing that you already don't have, all they can do is to tell you to find out for yourself, do your own investigation, find out who you are. No one can wheel you into heaven, you must enter on your own, by your own investigation.

38

It's All Junk

So now lets go back to the apparent Awakening, when one has Awakened to the truth of their Being, the light that has been smeared over with illusionary junk is now beginning to clear. Everything that had you under the illusion is now being revealed, there still will be illusionary habits appearing but now they are noticed, as before they were hidden in the psyche. These hidden illusions that are now revealed will gradually decline just like a black cloud slowly moving to reveal the sun behind it.

At this time we can even feel bored, this is because the ego is stirring and bringing up all that made it happy, it could be something like the path, the victim, it can be anything at all as long as it gets your attention.

It's like any addiction when we try to give it up, the receptors are screaming out for their fix, in the case of the ego it can even be worse, after all it's the whole psyche that is screaming out. The good news now is that because the light has now being allowed to shine within, all that is stirred is now Realised for what it is, just junk. This junk is being let go of because now you see it as junk where as before you were holding onto it not realising it to be junk.

Just like a house that you are cleaning out for a spring cleaning, it takes some time to have it all sparkling and clean. This parasite, the ego, has been living in you for a very long time, the light that is now coming in and revealing this parasite to you, is becoming stronger and stronger, soon there will be no room for the ego for the light will fill your whole being. You can then say as Jesus was reported to say, "I am the light of the world", for that's what we are, pure light, coagulated light.

So be reassured that when this light is allowed to enter your whole being that you will be purified, your heart centre will be activated and from there you will see the world as it really is, you will see that there is no good and bad, that all there is, is ignorance. The people out there who are doing these so called bad things are only still asleep, they don't Realise who they hurt, is really their self. Again this is what Jesus meant when the Romans were crucifying him, "Father forgive them for they know not what they are doing". This is true compassion, to see the other as your SELF, faultless and free.

Some say that you must be under grace to come to this Realisation, but the truth is we are all under grace, as we are also pure Awareness, we need to go within and take our gift of grace, it's there like any other gift, all we need to do is open them. We need to stop thinking that others have something that we don't, that Jesus has something that can never be reached, that the Buddha is the only one who has obtained true Buddhahood. We are told this by insecure people who have tried to reach their true SELF and never could, if they cannot, no one will and that is how they want it to be.

Of course this is all bullshit, our true Being is who we are, it's our birth right, we need to leave these institutions with their insecure beliefs and move onto higher things that we are meant to be in. Once we have discovered our higher Being, then we will really know how to live, then we can say as Paul did, "I live, yet not I, but Christ liveth within me".

39

The Truth Can Never Be Labelled

When I say that you cannot do anything about it, that you cannot destroy the ego, what I am saying is that while you are still in the mind you will only use that against itself, so the enemy is fighting the enemy. Now if the enemy wins over the enemy, what do we have left, of course we have the enemy, so you see its just futile to even try. This is what happens when one goes to a belief system that teaches from the mind, it will teach you that you must believe in order to win over the mind, that you must believe in a saviour to be saved. This can never happen until you give up all beliefs and enter within your own Being, there you will find the inner Saviour—you really can only help yourself when you drop your false self, the ego.

Beliefs will keep you in a place where you will feel comfortable, but you will never grow from there, you will be like a Bonsai tree. Yes, your beliefs will be beautiful to look at but that's all they will ever be, you will miss out on your full inner growth, you will never see your full inner Being. You will label your beliefs and fight for them to protect them, but truth can never be labelled because truth is ever flowing, it is not a stagnant pool of water, it is the Ocean, it is all that there IS.

Beliefs are conditioning, we hear them from others and take them on board for our own, they are packaged for us and we need not do anything but to just believe them. Our growth is halted and we then stop growing, we continually feed on these beliefs forever trying to find more beliefs to solidify the ones we all ready have.

So to go beyond the beliefs we must inquire to what truth is, not to believe in truth but to go into it and experience it for ourselves, when you go within and experience silence for your self you cannot then come back and package this silence, it can only be experienced from within. All beliefs are nothing but lies formulated by the mind, all what I have said also should not be believed in. Truth is Self discovery, it's your individuality which of course is everyone else's individuality, but still it must be experienced by your own inner witnessing, not from someone else's hearsay.

So I or anyone else cannot offer you anything but to point you in your own direction, then from there you must question who you are. If you find who you are then find where you are, if you find where you are then ask am I transient or am I infinite, keep questioning who you are until you find who you truly are. Don't listen to what others say you are or tell you what you are not—this is only second-hand knowledge, someone else's beliefs—find your own truth, until you do you will never be happy, that is, truly happy.

When you do find your inner Being and for the first time Realise who you are, only then will you really know the truth and this truth cannot be argued over by anyone else, for this is your truth, your inner experience, how could anyone argue with you when they haven't realised your inner truth. You will find that those who have disappeared into their inner Being will not want to argue with you, because they understand exactly what you are talking about, they have been there, they are your true brothers and sisters in Christ or Consciousness, they are home where you are.

So why do I sound like I am contradicting myself by saying that I have nothing to give you, and at the same time give you pointers that you can follow. Well because one is still in the belief that they are of the mind body, they can only understand from that point of reference, so there needs to be an understanding from this point of view, so as to at least bring the mind to a rest. If one goes into the silence within and goes gracefully into this silence, then teachings or pointers have done their work. From this silence that has at least brought the mind to a less restless state, one can now through Self-Inquiry enter their true Being, where as before not knowing anything at all about their true inner Being, one would have just stayed in their ignorance.

Our efforts can only take us so far, they can only take us to the edge of the river, we can only cross when we drop all efforts and beliefs, this other side of the river cannot receive anything that is transitory, in fact it cannot receive anything of you but your true Essence, your true Being.

If we are still attached to worldly things at this stage of transition, we will not totally disappear into pure Being on the other side of the river. The other side of this metaphorical river is likened to the veil that separates us from our true Being or home. This veil is only an illusion, its tapestry made from our life's accumulated programming and conditioning. As the story of Jesus said, when Jesus died on the cross the veil in the most holy place of the earthly sanctuary was ripped from top to bottom, this means that when we go beyond the mind body, beyond its illusions, the veil of separation is ripped down and our true nature is revealed in all its Glory. In this Glory we Realise that we are ONE with what is beyond the illusionary veil—all Now has been revealed, all Now is ONE.

Many teach that we are God, but the problem with this is that the one who is declaring that they are God, is in most cases not at the stage where they are truly Realised, so what they are saying is still coming from the ego's point of view. So to say that one is God needs more inquiring to who is this God, is it the mind body, is it my individual self as the ego? We need to strip of all that we are not, to reveal who we truly are, and then from there, yes we can declare that I AM GOD.

When one has disappeared into this Oneness and has realised what IS, then from there One can see that all is One, that there is only ONE GOD, there is no need to declare that you are this God. Do you need to declare that you are a human being? Of course not, so to say that you are God after the Realisation that you and everything that is, then it really makes no sense. There are many that only really want this so called Enlightenment for the happiness that they believe it will bring, of course there is total happiness in Oneness but again it is who you are already. You can only be still and Know that you are pure Happiness, or God, it's all the same. So if you are just after true happiness then you might miss it, because you will want this happiness and because of the wanting which is still from the minds point of view, you will not enter true happiness. You may find happiness but it won't be unique, it will fade just like all the other things of the mind that you've been chasing.

40

False Pleasure

This true happiness that many are longing for is sought after in various ways, such as money and power, relationships, self importance and so on—the list is endless—but until we drop all outer clinging we will never find this sought after happiness. We must also realise that happiness is just a concept of past conditioning, we have labelled what we have experienced as happiness, we have totally lost what once was an inner true happiness that we experienced as a child. Small children are naturally happy but unfortunately this is also changing, today children are forced to so-called grow up faster than ever, they are also becoming materialistic in their wanting to be happy, where as in the not long ago past they were left to grow up in their own time and space.

So really, behind all that we do, is the wanting to be happy. We are as the mind body organism pleasure spongers, soaking up as much pleasure as we can, there's nothing wrong in wanting to have pleasure, but it becomes suffering when we are addicted to this so called pleasure. There is nothing wrong in eating, we need to eat so as to sustain the body, but eating can be confused with true happiness, and because of this there are many who are morbidly obese, and many also die because of this. Of course overeating is only one small area of this illusionary happiness, this illusionary happiness is never satisfied because like all that is sort after on the outside, be it eating, sex, or whatever, it can never satisfy our inner Being, or should I say our inner happiness. I have since my apparent Awakening, come to be happy with all that I do, or all that I don't do. The drive to find happiness outside of myself is still there, but this drive is from Knowing that all outside of myself is all illusionary compared to what Is.

So in the pleasure of what is out there is seen for what it is, just like when we go to watch a good movie, we enjoy the movie fully but we also know that the movie is not real, so we don't go through the rest of our lives upset by the movie, because it was a sad movie of someone dying.

The outside so called world is for us to enjoy, after all we are the One who made this world to be enjoyed through the mind body organism, just as all animals also clearly enjoy their life on the outside. When we Realise this we can then balance the two worlds, not going over too far to the other, and getting lost there, and never experiencing the pleasure of the other.

Yes we can get caught up in being too introverted or extroverted and miss the whole point of our true existence. When we become Awakened to our true nature and the light is now on, everything is clearly seen for the first time, and a whole new world is there for us to explore. We are as little children again, not as spoiled, or materialistic over stimulated, but just with innocence that loves to explore the wonders of the world outside and inside.

This is how I felt when all was revealed, everything looked as new, just simple things like looking at a tree or smelling a flower, even watching people go by doing their own thing, all now looked as new. All Now is seen as the Awakened, even though most don't realise this, still, all I could see was the Awakened and they were and are still beautiful to behold. For they all collectively, are as I Am also, as I am them, and we are altogether.

Why are there some that are after this Enlightenment and at the same time will try to tear down whatever pointers are offered to them? If there are others that have entered this beautiful Being, they try to tear them down to where they are, it's as if they don't want another being there before they can even get a leg in the metaphorical door. Again this is the ego believing that its got to be its way, or no way at all, it is on an narrow path and refuses to see those around it who may be there already.

They are usually those who are too far into their minds, they try to intellectualise all that they know instead of dropping all that they know and just simply enter within. You also hear these same people say that those who are giving pointers, or may have a number of books, or charge for Satsang, are not really Awakened, if they were why would they charge money? Haven't they heard that we need money to by food and shelter—even the Enlightened Being has to live and also enjoys buying things for their enjoyment. This is nothing but an excuse by the ego mind to keep you on your miserable path, a path that will never lead you anywhere but to your own insecurities. I have noticed this on a Spiritual Forum where I tried to share what I have experienced or what I have apparently experienced. These very people will jump out of the woodwork, and jump up and down screaming blue murder, instead of listening to what I was sharing and realising that I wasn't saying that I had anything that they don't have already. They just try to make what is said chaotic, and by doing so they take away from others that may be ready just to hear one pointer, to make them explode into Being, these are the ones that are like dynamite, as apposed to those who are more like dry wood where they need just a little more pushing. But the one who comes in fighting and screaming are more like damp wood, no matter what they hear it is never going to do anything, they are too full of themselves, they have accumulated too much that it drowns any truth that comes their way.

These are like the fundamentalists who believe that they already know everything that needs to be known and because of this there is no room for anything new—their cups are too full to take anything within that may ignite their inner Being. This is the funny thing about when we are Awakened to what IS, you'll find that the world cannot understand you, for how can the outer understand what is within. My advice to you who have Awakened to what IS, is to for awhile keep what you have discovered to your self, keep it there until there are those that you meet who you know are ready to hear this inner Knowledge, knowledge that can never be found outside your self. With this inner Knowledge you don't feel that you have something that nobody out there doesn't already have, it doesn't come from the ego wanting nothing but praise, no, it comes from a place of pure Love and compassion. This is why you want to share this with all out there so that they will also at last know of their true inner Being, their true SELF.

When Jesus started to share his inner Being with those around him, the Pharisees strait away wanted to knock him down to their level, a level that has never been within and discovered their true Being, a level that will never Know of true Love, and even today they haven't really found this true Love, this is why they are still fighting today a useless war that nobody will ever win.

41

Inner Transformation

So lets talk about Christianity, there are so many professing to be Christians and believe that they have the answers from their Divine book called the bible. They believe that they are the only ones who know how to read this book, and from there they have made hundreds of churches all believing in a slightly different version, so which one is correct. Well there is no need to find out which is true or not, you cannot tie truth up in a package and hold it in a church, no church could ever hold the truth, all that a church can do to truth is kill it. Yes to know Christ, their so called saviour is to Know your true inner SELF, but the many that are clinging to Jesus as their saviour are missing the whole point of the teaching supposedly told by this man.

Many are also clinging to a future Christ that is going to come again and save them from this world, in most cases the world really needs saving from these people who can be potentially dangerous. Most of Christianity is actually anti-Christ, they believe in this man called Jesus and by clinging onto this man they never go further than this, they never really mature Spiritually, they are still greedily wanting this man to do it all for them They are told that to do anything for themselves is from the devil. They are right in a small way but they are completely missing the whole point, what they are missing is their inner transformation, which Jesus himself talked about, and because of this clinging, they have completely missed what Jesus was trying to say.

If we look at the scriptures as something apart from ourselves then that's what we will see, separation between our self and what we call God. For too long now Christianity has looked at God as separate from themselves. They have begged their so called God for everything as if he's a Father Xmas. There is no one out there for you to beg to so you may as well give in to the whole stupidity, and realise that you are already everything out there and everything that is not out there.

What is the use of praying to a God to feed the hungry when all you do is sit on your backside, if that is what you want then do it yourself somehow. Yes this is a very lazy organisation where much praying happens but not much more, they go to church every week asking for forgiveness, feeling that they are now safe for another week. When they realise that there is no one to forgive, that there is only ignorance of who they truly are, then and only then will they start to grow Spiritually, then they will Realise that they are the Christ which dwells within each and every person on the face of the earth, then will the true Christ rain on the earth, then will the true second coming of Christ be for everyone that has realised this from within.

So many are wasting their lives waiting for this event in time, its never going to happen, at least not outside of you, as Paul said again, "I live yet not I but Christ liveth within me". Jesus the man made what we are within, personified, but unfortunately most do don't see this for what it is, and because of this they have missed out on their true inheritance, they have bypassed their whole Being and missed out on a life of beauty and guilt free, no more to beg for anything from a man made God.

It really doesn't matter what religion you are in, if you keep your eyes on the centre of the teachings, this will bring you to your true Self in the end, also religion such as Christianity can be a great stepping stone as it was in my case.

As I said earlier in the book I came to a stage where the teachings of my church could not really take me any further, I knew within that

I wanted to grow but just couldn't, so this is why I left the church. My church brought me to Christ but that was it, it kept me away from wanting to be as Christ, in fact this was seen as blaspheming God, where now I see, to be kept away from becoming the Christ, is to be the anti-Christ, or you could also say it is blaspheming Christ not to become your true Self, the Christ.

The Christ is our mediator to God the father, it's our connection via the mind body, but it must be seen that the Christ is not to be taken literally. It is just a word that points to our higher Consciousness, even though it is called our mediator the reality is that there is only ONE, the Christ and the Father are not separate, while there is the mind body we see it as such from that perspective.

When one is Awakened to their true nature then the concept of the Christ and even the Father are also dropped, in this pure Being there is no concepts at all regarding any level in Consciousness or God, the mountains and valleys have all become One level. There are many who are drawn to religion for the social side, and of course there is nothing wrong with that, but then there are those who are hungry for the centre truth, they have an inner longing to be home but in their earlier stage they are confused where this home is. These are the ones where organised religion can stunt their growth, it teases them by bringing them so far and leaving them there, it teaches them to keep studying the same level over and over again, never allowing them to move on from there.

The reason they don't want them to move on is because they themselves don't know how to move on. This conscious or unconscious fear wants to keep close to the numbers and is too frightened to move forward, many teach that to go forward is to be under the influence of the so called devil. This all seems so childish to the one who as adventured out and found their true Being. They look back and feel with compassion for those who are kept behind in an institution of fear. Why is there this fear? The fear is there because these people are still in heir minds, they are teaching from their minds only. To teach from within the heart is too fearful for the ego, the ego is too afraid to be found out, and when found out the ego loses its power over you.

The death of the ego or mind is the end of the one who has refused to grow, but the thing is this is what Jesus taught all along. The crucifixion was a symbol for the death of the ego mind body, the story of the cross wasn't told to keep you in guilt over the death of Jesus for the rest of your life—it has nothing to do with this man Jesus dying on a cross or not—its all to do with you. It's your story, you are the one the story is all about not someone who supposedly lived over 2000 years ago. You are the one who must die to be renewed in you true SELF the Christ, to leave the old man behind, he was never you in the first place, so now it's time to stop giving him first place in your life and move on.

42

Spiritual Discernment

So whatever belief you have, no matter how beautiful it is it is still just a belief, and all beliefs are from the mind trying to make sense of what it cannot understand. The belief that we may have will give us a false sense of security, we need to add to the belief so as to prove to ourselves that our belief is rock solid.

Just stop and think, if you knew that your beliefs were rock solid, would you bother trying to protect them, why would you if you knew they were totally true without flaw. Awareness has nothing to do with believing, its just what IS, it's not a thing you can grasp and hold dearly to yourself, its all that there IS. You cannot package awareness and sell it from a church, it's there free for the taking, its what we are, Totally. All I can do is point you to it and then its up to you to let go and just disappear into it, from there you will have an inner knowing of what IS, the light will be turned on and all will be revealed, but try to explain what this inner Knowing is and you will find no words to describe it. For this reason it has been hinted at, and as Jesus taught in parables so as not to over stimulate the ego mind, by revealing the truth within the story or a parable the inner child comes to hear the stories, just as children likes to hear stories told to them before bedtime by their parents.

These stories or parables then excite the inner innocence of the childlike mind, and they are thought upon without the ego trying to work it out for its own egocentric greediness. When the ego mind pretends to find the truth, it doesn't want to find the truth to realise its true Self, or its true nature, to do so, it knows very well that it will mean its death.

This is what has happen to the world scriptures, they have been argued over and over by those who believe they know best, they have also been added to and subtracted from leaving nothing of its true originality. For this reason we need to use Spiritual discernment to even come close to what the original pointers were pointing to, behind all this chaos over many years with the scriptures, was non other than the very ego centred mind, which tried to hide as much as possible from the many people, who in those times were never educated and had no idea of what was happening. This is one reason also why the early church gave their sermons in Latin, and wrote only a small number of bibles in Latin also. The innocent public had no idea what was being said and most could not read—these were the dark ages, an age where so many were kept in ignorance.

Without the brave few who started to question those times, like discovering that the earth was not the centre of the universe, and many other discoveries that went against the established beliefs of the Roman church, we would be still in this God fearing hell on earth. It's no wonder that the people of the day believed in such superstitions as the devil and eternal hell. In most areas around the world we are now free to choose and discover our own truths, but yes the ego is still alive and well, but in a more subtle way, even though everything looks so wonderful on the surface, underneath it all and especially in organised religions, the ego mind is working towards bringing as many as it can to a belief system, that will keep the multitudes asleep and away from ever finding their true Nature, which will be the end of the established belief systems forever.

The words that I have conveyed throughout this book may have been a bit too direct for some, but I do not like sugar-coating words just to have the reader continuing to read on, or just for the hope that I am going to tell them what they want to hear. There are plenty of books out there to do that for you if that's what you want, but sugarcoating the truth is never going to be any good to you, unless you want to stroke the ego and keep it happy. When one is searching for the truth they are still asleep, for if they had Realised the truth they wouldn't be searching, for this reason I don't like to over emotionalise the words that I use to point with. To do so only keeps one on the so called path. There are many who just love to read the scriptures because of the beauty of the words, and they can be beautiful to read, but until you move on from the words and transcend to where they are pointing, that's where you will stay. Of course if that is where you like to stay, that's well and good but for the serious seeker of truth, it just won't do, for you I hold back on offering you something that I can never provide, all I can offer is my own story and my own pointers that may or may not help you.

If this so called Awakening was that simple, that anyone could just read a few words and there and then be Awakened, then everyone would be there, or should I say everyone would be right where they already are, but Realising it. I think if Jesus' words were more direct with not so much sugar-coating on them, there may have been more Awakened even sooner, but as I said earlier maybe the ego would have taken it on board for itself and missed the whole point. But we are here over 2000 years away from what was said then, and I am not going to sugar-coat my words to keep others on another 2000 year sleeping voyage. There are those also who take offence to hearing about the ego being ignorant, they believe they are the ego, not Realising that the ego is just an illusion. They also don't realise that they are already there and all they have to do is drop this very thing that they are upset about. These are the people who want their ego's stroked and pampered, they are not ready to be Awakened and only want to be because they want what is to them, something that is hard to obtain, and this is a challenge for the ego and the ego loves a challenge.

So understand that this is not hard, again and again I say to you that you are there already, yep, there I go again, in fact if you are still heavily under the influence of the ego, you probably would have stopped reading this book by now. So lets assume that those of you who are still reading this book, have dropped the ego or at least diminished it to some degree. Well here I must say to you that you still haven't really let these words point you totally to your true Source.

Don't forget what I have been saying right throughout this book, that there is no ego, it's all an illusion, but still you cannot really see this, so do you see the power we have given to this illusion? As I have said, there is only ONE power, all other power no matter what it is, is still also only an illusion, the illusion that you believe that there is power outside of your Being. Even to the Awakened this illusion still arises, but when you are Awake to this, its there and gone, you just don't cling to it like you once did, for how can you cling to an illusion.

43

See Beyond the Words

What I should add at this point is that there are those who believe that when they are Awakened that there is much more to do, as if you have only seen a small piece of light through a crack in Consciousness, again this is only the ego trying to take them away from even this small crack of light that they believe they have seen. When there has been this disappearance into pure Being, there is nothing more to be seen, its either you have been there or you haven't, you cannot just peep through into your Being and say that you are half Awakened, it's just too silly for words.

No matter what you believe you have found, while you are still out there trying to find what IS, no matter how much of what IS you believe you have seen, you're still playing the game of being lost and still trying to find home. So its either you are home, or you're not and if you're not, then you are still under the influence of the illusionary ego mind. You are still seeing what is within you as something you still need to work on but there is nothing to work on, all you can do is let go and let God, when you give all to your true Being to God, you then are no longer working by the sweat of your brow. But now all you are doing is living in the Realisation that you need not do nothing, but to rest in the arms of your father, for he doeth all the works from now on.

You were the prodigal Son or Daughter but now your father has received you back into His arms and there you will forever be. You see how these few words that I have just used from the New Testament, describes our Oneness with our true Being or Self so beautifully, so yes there are many beautiful words throughout the Scriptures. As I said earlier we have to move on from the words, and go direct to where the words are pointing to, then when we have entered our true home, then we can come back to the words and really see them for the first time like we have never seen them before. When you do start to see the scriptures come alive you will then wonder why you have never noticed them as you do now, of course again it's the old villain, the ego.

This illusionary ego that clouds our minds has kept us away from really seeing the world as it is, it has caused us to see everything as a label, like a filing cabinet we keep referring to over and over to obtain a label for everything we see, hear, smell, feel and even taste. There are times when one becomes Awakened that they can actually for the very first time experience all the senses as new, if one was addicted to something like alcohol or smoking, or whatever, after the Awakening they now seem to have no interest in them.

I remember when I used to get drunk every weekend, but after the apparent Awakening over night it just vanished, in fact I cannot even drink alcohol, even if I wanted to, it just makes me sick. Like all addictions we are only using them to cover up something in our lives that we are not happy with. I drank because I wasn't happy, then again after the Awakening I was full of inner happiness, a happiness that I have never known before. This happiness that comes from within our very Being, and once discovered, will never leave you again, even in sad times it's still there just sitting in the background letting you know that it hasn't gone anywhere.

Throughout these writings I have been trying to avoid quoting what others have said of their own Awakening experience, after all they wouldn't be my own experience so I wouldn't have any idea what they experienced, all experiences are secondary to what IS. When there is this disappearing into Being there is no one there to experience anything but Being its SELF, what we call the experience is what arises through the mind body. The purer the mind the purer the experience, if the mind is still muddy with the ego residue then this will come through with the experience, but of course if one has Awakened then the mind would be at a purer quality, for if it wasn't there would have been no Awakening in the first place.

So no matter what scriptures or writings of anyone you read its never going to be what IS, you will have to Realise that for your SELF, then you too will then have your own experience of what IS. But again your experience won't be what IS either, you can only use your experience as a pointer for others and so it goes on and on, all a beautiful tapestry of Awakened experiences. Jesus was reported to say that, I am the way, the truth, the light, now to realise this truth you must Realise it from your SELF, reading these words will never transform you, you must become the truth, the way, the light, then you will Know from within what He meant, it has now become your own inner Truth.

You see truth is nothing to be gotten or to be found, it's who you are, its what everything IS, as soon as you grab a piece of abstract from the mind you have lost what truth is, it cannot be conceptualised, again it can only be another pointer. When one fully Realises this there are no more questions on what is truth, it has now been realised from within your inner Being, there is no question of what it is from there. When you are not coming from your inner Being, then again you are outside looking in, trying to find it all over again. You see all that I have said is from my own perspective, from my own inner intuition, but what is on the other side of this intuitive language is nothing but pure silence, pure Consciousness, there are no words or thoughts in Consciousness, so when it is allowed to arise in its purity, it then comes through the mind and then is spoken or written by the inspiration of God.

This is how we have so many scriptures throughout the world, they have been written by the one who have entered their true Being, and allowed this pureness to arise through the mind that has been purified of its garbage. Again the mind is neutral, it allows the thoughts to come to surface, so we as the mind body needs to decide what to do next, but we have polluted the mind over time with unnatural thoughts derived from the illusionary ego, the mind that once served us has now become our enemy. Of course this enemy is all illusionary and we as the mind cannot get rid of it, so here we are again asking how do we get rid of this illusionary ego mind? Again we can't, we can only see for what it is and from there just drop it, let it go and stop owning it, stop dressing it up and sugar-coating it, it's sour and can never be made sweet, as your true Being is.

Puppet On A String

> *Every thought you have makes up some segment of the world you see. It is with your thoughts, then, that we must work, if your perception of the world is to be changed.*

ACIM

So now you realise that you are not your mind body and also you are not your thoughts, that is your thoughts when you are not in line with your true Being. When you do become in line with your true being your mind then becomes purer, your thoughts now are coming from a deeper place and also your thoughts now are not tainted with the illusionary ego garbage.

When the ego mind is quietened you then allow the pure thoughts that are arising from your Being, not that pure Being has words within it to be heard. Because you are a mind body organism that was made through pure Being, and now you are allowing for the first time your true inner thoughts that are pure and innocent, they are no more pulled out of a programmed mind that has been conditioned to say what it was programmed to say.

Before you were like a puppet moved by the strings of the ego, but now you are finally in charge of the whole event of your human adventure, now you can really enjoy being a human being and not wasting the life that you entered through Consciousness. Also remember that the body is within you, within your pure Being, when the body is more you are still where you always have been, you haven't gone anywhere. So just keep reminding yourself over and over that you are pure Being, animating through your mind body but also don't forget to be balanced, you have made this wonderful body of yours to enjoy this life, so enjoy it.

When we are balanced and living in harmony with nature, for that is who we are as a mind body organism, nature. We then find that life will also move in harmony with us, we no longer see out there as something to fight against. We start to accept things a lot better and no longer see ourselves as victims of the world, of course there are going to be the same hardships but we won't be over taken by them, we won't let them become a neurosis that over takes our whole life.

Even when death comes we will greet it as our friend and not as an enemy, we will still miss our loved ones but we will miss them because of who they were, and not let their passing keep us from moving on and still enjoying our life that we still have to live out. As more and more become Awakened we may shift away from the world that we know now, we may become less materialistic, we may plan our children a lot better and let them grow as children, not trying to push them into a life that they were never meant to live. We now teach our children that we are all One and no one is above the other, they will grow without peer pressure or trying to be in the 'in' crowd wearing what the cool kids are wearing. We may seem to those who are still asleep as if we are going backwards instead of forwards but to the Awakened it will be the complete opposite, backwards will be forwards.

There will be no name for this way of living, it won't be capitalism or communism, it will be just simply living together in an Awakened state. When we see others who are struggling in life, who are starving or whatever, we will be there as a family not as an institution waiting for money hand outs, we won't waste so much money on our space projects, we will look after our own planet first and foremost.

Sticky Love

1 John 4:8

He that loveth not knoweth not God; for God is love.

So we are back to this sticky word *Love*, if God is love and God wants us to be love, to love each other as we love ourselves then we must also be this love, for how could we love another if we weren't? For God to want us to be love and if we weren't love, then how on earth could we love, it would be like asking a robot to love another robot. This is where many go wrong in believing that God is separate from us, with this belief it is impossible to ever love another, or ourselves even. So when one becomes Awakened to what IS, one then Realises that we are all One, we are all God, we are Love.

Now this is a whole different story, here now we have our SELF, which is the same SELF as every one else's SELF, so now you can see what these words of John's are trying to explain, we also now can see clearly what love is. It's no longer separate as we were led to believe, especially by organised religion that only wants to keep us within their flock of people, begging for this love from a separate God.

When I came to realise this from within I could feel this love for the first time, I would look at strangers just walking past and feel an inner connection. They were strangers but they felt like family, where as before family was just something that I was born into and was supposed to be above all else, others were out there, my family was in here with me. Of course we see our blood relationships as being close but only because we are closer to them, we know them much more than others. But if you were born into any other family you would feel the same way with them, no matter where they are in the world. So we are much more than just blood relationships, we were born into these families but we are always beyond these families.

We are all One in Consciousness or God, we are Consciousness animating through all these families that seem to be separate, just as the electricity running through all the appliances, all the appliances cannot work without that one electrical energy.

So here we are born into a family, we are named by this family's surname that has been handed down over many years, we then are given a first name that we are known by and we are even given a middle name, or even more names to add to our identity. What our parents have learnt about life thus far is also added to our life story, so now we treasure this information that we have learnt about this family that we are now part of, and God help anyone who tries to interrupt this organisation.

This family extends out to what culture and country that we may be in, this also becomes part of our story and again God help anyone who says anything about our country or culture, and so we have wars to take care of this.

Yes, true Love is nothing to do with a relationship but it can be what the relationship is built on, the under foundation that keeps it together, this ever flowing stream or foundation is our true Being, it is the ocean that everything is within. When we become and allow ourselves to emerge back into this ocean, that we left through the illusionary ego, then there will be truly peace on earth, when we all can live in harmony and true love.

So, where are we now, we have seen that we cannot do nothing to obtain Enlightenment, we have realised that we are that already, we have seen that all we can do is just give into Being and be still in the silence within. This is as far as any pointer can direct you and this is the reason why so many believe they can go no further. Many try to go into the silence and from there they try even harder to obtain this silence but the harder you try the more you are lost within the mind.

You cannot try to be silent, you can only let go of trying and rest in the arms of silence, just give into it and the silence will do the rest for you—silence will be your catalyst changing you from the ego mind to the Godly mind that you truly are. The Godly mind isn't someone who thinks that they are above others, it doesn't think its more purer than others, it just Realises that you and every one else are the same, and with this realisation there is a tremendous love overflowing in compassion for all. This overflowing love sees all as Awakened, it doesn't see the ignorance that is causing the blindness, it just sees the beautiful radiance of God shining through all.

I remember before the Awakening I saw the world as a frightening place, maybe because of the so called bad things that happened to me throughout my life, but now everything changed, all I see out there now is a beautiful world full of beautiful people and not just people but animals and also inanimate objects, that we still are part of. When we are One with all again, when we are in touch with our true Being, we feel then as if we don't have a skin that separates us from the outside world, we now feel as if we are extended throughout the whole Cosmos. Of course we need to remind ourselves that there is still this mind body organism that we are animating through, and this is where we need to keep the balance, we still need to render onto what belongs to the outside world. Our true treasures are within or if you like in heaven, our inner sanctuary is our dwelling place away from the hustle and bustle of the egocentric world of ignorance.

Now when we see the outer world caught up in its neurotic dreams we know that that isn't what it is, what we are seeing is just an illusionary projection, projected by the many who are still asleep. This sleeping world needs a lot of love and understanding, which should only come through compassion. Through compassion we can extend our love through every man and woman and child, only through this love can mankind be Awakened from their dream.

How can we do this in our everyday life? Well when someone comes to you who are lost in their dream and is talking about how bad the world is, just stop them and remind them about all the beauty in the world, that there is far more greater good in the world than so called evil, remind them to not let the media control their minds, not to let them magnify a small pocket of trouble into a world calamity. But we must do this in love and not force this upon others for they will attack you for doing so, after all no one wants to be awakened from sleep. Just subtly remind them that everything is ok, there is no reason to panic, there is no reason to live in fear, the only thing to fear is fear itself and even that is an illusion.

46

Inner Magnetism

As you are reading these words keep remembering that is all they are, just words. Let the words lead you to where they will, within your own Being, don't try to analyse them or philosophise them, this will only keep you in the mind, for the mind loves to analyse and pull apart everything that comes its way.

Of course we still need to question all that comes our way but only that which takes us away from our SELF. When you hear words that point you to what IS you'll have an inner Knowing that this is the way to go. Many feel this when for the first time they come into contact with a Master, there's an inner magnetism that remembers its SELF, when it is close by to that which it IS. This inner SELF that has been called all sorts of names isn't what IS either, I know I have said over and over that we need to dissolve into our true Being, but again even this isn't what IS, how can we in all truth dissolve into what we already are.

I need to remind you over and over for the simple reason that the ego being manipulative and cunning, will grab onto anything at all to keep you from finding who you truly are. We need not find a Master to be drawn into Being, we can also find this in books, the words in the book that have been written by the one who has tasted this inner Awareness, has within their pages this magnetism also that draws us to our true Being.

Just as music can draw us to feel certain emotions from the past such as sad times or good times, the music sets off memories that are stored in the unconscious and brings them to the conscious mind. In this way also there are truths that reawaken what has been laying dormant within our spiritual being, these truths Awaken the memory of our connection with God, we have become again the begotten of the father, and all because we were drawn back to Him through our inner magnetic love for Him. Just as Jesus said before he died on the cross, "It is finished", we can say also with all honesty, now, that it is finished, that we are Home at last.

When we have arrived we now for the first time, understand what the scriptures were saying, in fact we see truth all around us, we can even see it in what is called evil, there is nowhere that it isn't found for all is One in God. We need to remind ourselves each day where we are Now. Again as Paul the Apostle said "I die daily", we are renewed from the old man to the New man.

It has taken many programmes and conditioning to where you are now, and it will take a small time now that you have Awakened to put all this into perspective. Now you are no longer under the influence of the ego that made all your decisions for you, based on its neurotic behaviour, of false knowledge that it was building its whole life on. Now your decisions are made on what you now feel intuitively within, its like a little voice that seems to know what needs to be done for the best, as before the voice was only thinking of itself, this is because it wasn't coming from a higher place but from the depths of your lower mind, a mind that was polluted by years of conditioning, a mind that was deluded by the illusionary ego. Now the mind is becoming your friend, it is now a fine instrument to help you through your life as a human being, a human being that now enjoys its life as it was meant to be enjoyed.

47

The Awakened Life

Now that we are Awakened we now live our life in Awareness, where as before we were living our life in a dream, a dream that we thought was real. In this Awareness we see for the first time the beauty all around, yes it was there before but now its for real, we look at the sunset without naming it or comparing it to past sunsets, we just see what IS. Because of the conditioning we are taught from childhood what everything is, we are taught what colours are, we are taught what labels to attach to everything, and of course we do need a system where we all can agree on what we are observing, but that's all it is, it should be used for convenience and that's where it should end.

When we are observing for ourselves, we should be aware of what we are observing from an inner connection to the very thing that we are observing, we are a part of whatever our senses comes in contact with. So now when we see a flower, we are the flower, the colour and the scent of the flower are part of our own vibration, even when we are eating we are now part of the food and the taste and even the smell, so now we are really enjoying what we are eating. People out there who we labelled as someone who we loved are now One with us, in this Awareness we are no longer separate but are joined together, and this is what is meant by being married, joined together. Of course you don't have to be married to be joined together, for we are all One already, marriage is only the recognition of this Oneness and so we share and celebrate it with our friends. Unfortunately too many see marriage as a binding law that two people should adhere by, and just as truth is destroyed by organising it, so is marriage.

When we live through Awareness we don't see the bad people out there as bad but just ignorant, now we send them healing and love instead of hate as we once did. We don't send them to prison just for revenge, we now send them there to teach them how to also realise their true Self, how can they learn about their ways if we treat them as criminals—they are also One with us and a prison cannot divide that.

Just by being more Aware everything will just fall into place on its own merit, greed will disappear because there is no one to be greedy in Awareness, it just cannot survive as any other traits that see others as someone to take advantage of. This all may sound like a pipe dream but as long as we think it cannot be reached, it will never be. The more we can help to Awaken, the more will Consciousness arise throughout the planet, this is already taking place right before us, many are realising that there's much more to life than fighting over it. Even though there is still a lot of materialism in the world, in some ways this is good, we may come to a point where because we had just about everything you can think of, we may come to the realisation that the simple things in life are much better.

We will gradually realise that all the things we wanted didn't bring us long lasting happiness, this will cause us to find where this true happiness comes from. There are many places throughout the world that are teaching people to find their true happiness, there are many Enlightened writers also teaching others to just let go and this happiness will automatically be there waiting for you, writers such as Eckhart Tolle, Tony Parsons, ACIM and many more are paving the road to this freedom that is just there waiting to be claimed.

48

Heaven Here, Now

Now heaven is established on the earth, heaven was never a geographical place somewhere in the sky, it was always here within you, now there is Awareness heaven is seen everywhere and in everything. There are so many waiting for heaven in a future dream, they spend all their life here praying to a God that they believe will allow them entry through the pearly gates, all this is just another dream to keep them away from ever knowing their true place which is heaven, here and Now.

Stop believing that you live in a sinful world and see your brothers and sisters as pure Being, stop seeing the outer shell and just see the radiance of pure love shining from within all. When you start to see this within all, you will stop fearing each other as your enemy, and now see all as your Self in Consciousness.

The belief in a future heaven is yet another greed cloaked in the belief in a loving God that will one day grant you this wish, so many are just following this belief hoping that when they die there will be something for them after death, all this is nothing more than fear and again because of the ego. This frightened ego will do anything to keep itself alive, death to the ego is the end of its life and so by believing in this future heaven, it brings relief to it so it can continue as the parasite that it is.

We don't have to try to change what's out there to be happy, all we need to do is change what is within, and out there will take care of itself. Out there is like the mind, It is neutral it is neither good or bad, when the mind is dirtied by the ego that's all we will see is a dirty world, learn to keep the mind neutral and the ego will have no chance to cling to it.

As long as we perceive the world out there separate we will always be living in fear of what is out there. When we finally Realise that we are everything out there, we then will not fear it because how can we fear what is our own Being? Fear is always from the past, it's our false conditioning that we project to the now and to the future, the fear of not reaching a geographical heaven is projected to now and the future, and all the time it has only kept us away from Realising that it is here NOW and within.

When I talk of illusion I am saying that this illusion is what keeps us from realising that we are One with all that IS, out there is there but it is all One, its when we see it as duality that we are caught up in the web of false belief, in fact its not even a belief, it is what IS, it needs no belief to make it so.

Never forget that all that I say is from dualism and because of this it should be seen as pointers only or metaphorically, of course I have to use language to communicate these words to you but always remember that there is only One reading these words.

We must also remember that whatever we perceive out in the world as beautiful or not, is still the illusionary shadow of what IS, for all out there is still within our Being and we are only seeing it as it is because of the mind body organism. Of course this is how it should be, after all, that is how the mind body works, but we must still realise this and also keep the balance that is needed for us to live a life that makes any sense.

Being Aware now doesn't mean that we all have to see the world the same as everyone else, what may be beautiful to one may not to another, so were not like robots as we were when lost in the dream of separation. We all have our own choices of what we like and what we don't care for, but behind all of this now we have the inner knowing that its all just an illusionary artistic play of Consciousness, and we now enjoy it for what it is.

So what is realised now is that we see the world all new, from what we thought we saw before this Realisation of what IS. Because of this it may take a small while to get our focus, so we can be balanced and not lose ourselves in either way, because we are living in this so called outer world there is an illusionary polar that we have to live with. The best way to do this is to keep in the middle, neither on either pole. But we still must live with two sides of the pole swinging, for this gives us movement where if this wasn't so everything would be in a static condition and there wouldn't be life at all.

There are lots of information out there on how to keep to this middle way of living, of course the first that comes to mind is the teachings of the Buddha. This way of living will certainly keep us balanced, there is also some good information from ACIM that will teach you how to live in the world in harmony, it uses the Christ within as our point of reference and how we are One with all that there is. It's good to read this information but we still should remember that all this information is still outside of our being, no matter where it comes from, for this reason we only use them as pointers, and when they have served their purpose we then put them away as we would with tools after using them.

It's also a good practice to remind yourself every day when you get out of bed who you truly are, that you are One with all that here IS, that you are Gods only begotten Son or Daughter, it doesn't matter, with God or your true inner Being there is no male or female, there is no duality at all.

Again we are like One big pot of stew without boundaries, even though there are the ingredients within the stew they are still the stew in its wholeness, we can taste or experience the so called ingredients as if there all separate but we know now that this is just Consciousness being the Cosmic Artist, its colour or medium being its many levels of vibration.

49

Trust in Life

So if it's security you want from life, well you are never going to find it. If you are expecting life to meet your demands then you are going against life itself, life is full of surprises and what we name those surprises means nothing to life, we are life itself and as soon as we realise this the better we well enjoy the life we are living, here, NOW. When we trust life and go with whatever may come we then free ourselves from the hold of the ego wanting its own way. Of course we can do things to make our life comfortable but we can only do what we can, and if there is nothing we can do then we should just trust in life to take care of itself, which we are part of also.

I remember once when I would be worried about all the mad prophecies that I read about, the church taught me to fear the future because the bible has predicted that the world was going to get really bad just before the second coming of Jesus. Because of my mental illness this made me feel even more frightened, there are many who believe this and because of this they are too frightened to question what the bible says, and at the same time they love this God who is going to destroy the earth, but their love is all to do with fear.

Fear controls everything outside of you, as long as you don't realise that you are more than what is out there you will fear what is out there. When you do realise that you are all that is out there and also what is not out there, your fear will then leave you because now you realise that there is really nothing out there to fear, the fear is only your perception of what you believe is out there.

As long as we believe that we are separate we will always be living in fear and insecurity, so the Enlightened one sees all as One and what is out there cannot harm us, even if we are killed by what is perceived to be out there. So what, we were never born and will never die, we are life itself were not going anywhere but where we are already, here, Now.

We will still try to avoid being hurt, like we won't just walk out on the road without looking first, after all we are created by our SELF to enjoy this life, what a waste if we foolishly end it just to prove that its not worth anything.

While we are believing we are separate from life we are putting ourselves in a prison, the only way out of this illusionary prison is Awareness. When we are Aware we then see that there was never a prison in the first place, we were always free. Now we see all others as free also, the world now isn't so frightening as we thought it was, fear is no longer our Awareness.

So Now we can get on with life and really enjoy it for the fi rst time, for fear is no longer our friend but its also not our enemy because it was always just an illusion, an illusion that kept us fearing our security.

So we are in the world but not of the world, all our inner beauty of pure love and true happiness are our treasures that are stored in heaven. This heaven is now seen from within and not in some distant future promise. We take from this supply of treasure that never empties, where as the illusionary things in the so called outer world only kept us amused for a short while.

It was never the things outside that brought us happiness, true happiness is not to be found outside but within our own selves. Love also was never to be found out there somewhere, we are love, its our pure Essence, it's the Source of all that there IS.

We are now seeing the world as it is, not with our physical eyes but with inner intuitional Knowing, we are much more than our five senses, these are only there to navigate us through the so called outer world, they are only useful as far as the mind body is concerned.

Beyond these senses we are all that there IS but within this pure Essence we cannot experience it as anything like we can with the five senses, it is converted into a concept as it arises through the mind body but again that isn't what IS, this is where the senses are not reliable to convey the truth to you and all we can do is use them as pointers.

When there is the apparent Awakening we begin to not be so bodily orientated, the mind also now is tamed and not so much a hindrance as it was when we were still asleep. Because the mind has been polluted over many years there will be some residue still there but this will now have no influence on our choices because now it's seen for what it is, the light has been switched on and what is still there is seen now to be only the illusion that it always was.

We live now without suffering, without the neurosis that controlled our life before, all this suffering was all because we believed that we were separate from everything out there. Because of the illusion of separation we tried to find our happiness out there, after all we thought that if we are separate we must get what's out there to feel complete. You don't need anything to be complete you are already complete, now there is Awareness you at last Realise this and your life Now is in harmony with all else.

This Awareness or Enlightenment was never waiting for anyone to arrive at its door, it wasn't waiting for anyone to even knock, in fact there was never a door there, so there was never a key needed to open it, you are the door, you are the key, you are Awareness its SELF.

When we are Awakened we no longer need to find out anything more, in fact there is nothing to find out, all you need to know is that you are it, you are pure Being, being Being, and all that's going on all around you is pure being also Being nothing more than Being. Now there's a whole new adventure waiting for you to explore and its all yours, so now play and enjoy your SELF.

50

Be the Lighthouse

Losing your identity is one thing that many are afraid of when they come to Awareness, they're too frightened to completely let go and disappear into their true Being, the thing is the identity that you believe is you is only the shadow of who you truly are. Your true Identity is Awareness and when we allow awareness to shine we live as who we truly are, you could say that we live now as the Christ, we are no longer the old man or carnal self.

We are now the light of the world and we should let our light shine, so that others can see us when they're upon the rough waters of the ocean, thrashing about and trying to swim or to control the rough waters, not Realising that *they* are the ocean and the rough waters that they are trying to control. We now stand out as the lighthouse for those who are ready to receive the truth and discover for themselves their true inner being.

The Enlightened one now sees all as the true Being and all that is needed is to remind the one who is seeking truth that they are already that which they are trying to find. Many will have a hard time realising this because they find it hard to realise that it could be so easy. After all some have been searching most of their lives, and for you to come along and tell them that they are already that, is not going to be accepted so easily, but all we can do is sow the seed and if the ground is by grace fertilised then the seed will grow, the ground being their inner readiness to receive the seed through grace.

To hide this wonderful Realisation that we have discovered, is very hard, because of the compassion that is so strongly pulling us to all those who are still asleep, the love within us is also recognising the love in everyone else. The Awakened one is more like the Ocean drawing all the rivers towards itself, the rivers being the ones out in the outer world trying to find their way back home to the Ocean.

We all now within our Awakening become as Saviours, not as one Saviour as most believe Jesus was, in all truth there is really only one Saviour, one Source, you your Self are your true Saviour, for there is really no one who can save you. You must disappear into your true Being alone, without anything clinging to you, not even the one that is already Awakened can bring you to your true SELF.

Also remember that as a Saviour its not what we can do to help others, but its where we can point those who are asleep. We of ourselves can do nothing, if one is Saved then it's because they were under grace and they only needed our presence and words that are from the Source its SELF. These words are now coming from a genuine experience in Consciousness, this is why they are loaded with such inner powerful magnetic force, that pulls towards its Self all that are lost in the rivers, trying to find the Ocean of truth, their true Home.

When we are Awakened there will be many out there who will try to challenge you, they will chellenge your disappearance into Being. You will find that those who are already Awakened will accept you as their Kindred in Spirit, the Awakened would not try to degrade your Awareness, why would they when they know now that everyone is already within Awareness.

There are many who are really trying to find this Awareness, and when they come across one that has disappeared into Consciousness, they cannot believe that you could possibly be there, for how could you be there when they're not? This is nothing more than the ego being jealous, it will always try to be one step ahead of everyone else, but while one is stuck with an ego that is so demanding to be Awakened, they will never be able to find their own inner Being.

The one who has Awareness doesn't need to protect their inner found truth, for how could we protect something that we all have.

There will be times especially just after the Awakening that the need to protect will arise, but this is only the residue of the ego, this need not bother you at all. Again just see it for what it is and move on from that illusionary thought, it is nothing more than remembered garbage that is still waiting to be cleared from the mind, for the mind will still take a little while to become purer.

There are some that believe that when there is an Awareness that they should be a pure Saint, or a pure Guru without blemish. This again is just the ego trying its best to pull everything around it down to its jealous level, when one is Awakened there is no such thing as rules to be adhered to, if there was then this again would only be because of the ego mind trying to pigeonhole what IS, into its own belief system of what isn't. This Awareness is not a competition of who can get there first, we are already there, we are only to remember that we are there, it's no big deal to the one who is truly Enlightened, its just a big deal to the ego that is chasing Enlightenment.

When you are ready to share your inner Being to others, share it with true Authority as Gods Beloved Son. If your inner Authority is taken as being arrogant by the ego mind of those who are still asleep, be not afraid of their accusations for they are only words coming from an illusionary ego mind, that is trying its hardest to bring you down and to even destroy you.

Never forget that it's not the person or the true identity of the person that is trying to attack you, the Love that is within all is only being overshadowed by the ego. The inner innocence of the person is who you should always see and nothing else, like Jesus who forgave the ones who were crucifying him because they were blind of their true inner Christ, so we who are Awakened should forgive also.

Now we look out into the world without judgment, we see for the first time others as our SELF, we don't see what is out there through conditioned glasses or even rose coloured glasses, for now there is nothing in between our inner vision, and what we do see is part of us also. We have spent so much of our life never really seeing what Is, we are so programmed and conditioned that what we do see is nothing more than what we have been told by others, we expect our loved ones to act in a certain way, we expect our relationships to also be in a way that we believe it should be, after all that's how they do it on the soapies on television.

When one has Awakened there can be a falling away from certain friends or even relationships, not because you now feel they're below you, for this would be still the ego, but because you no longer can be with someone's neurotic behaviour. Because they don't want to know what you have found it is better to walk away and let them be who they believe they are, for true love doesn't try to change anyone but lets them be who they want to be, after all they are pure Consciousness also, but only blind to it.

> *Even the very dust of your city, which cleaveth on us, we do wipe off against you: notwithstanding be ye sure of this, that the kingdom of God is come nigh unto you.*

Luke 10:11

> *If anyone will not welcome you or listen to your words, leave that home or town and shake the dust off your feet.*

Matthew: 14

When people that we come in contact with refuse to see that we have changed, and also refuse to try to realise that they too can Awaken, we should not be upset by this but to move on to the next opportunity. After all its not us that can change the other, it is God who triggers the heart to open and receive the truth of their inner Being to shine.

> *Jesus said, "Follow Me, and I will make you fishers of men."*

Mark 1: 17

Here Jesus is saying that when we become Awakened and ready to share our inner truth with others who are still searching, because you have been where they are, you realise that they also have the inner truth, for there is only One truth. So our job as the fisherman is to help to bring their inner being to surface, the inner Being is the deep truth like the fish who live deep within the Ocean. It's nothing to do with the mind that we are trying to bring to the surface, this has always been on the surface, this has been the false identity that we thought was us. When the deep truths are brought to the surface we see again the miracle of another beautiful Being, who now also shines with their inner truth. They have now also become the light of the world, as we Awaken from our dream we all continue on our way lighting more candles of truth, and because of this one day the earth will be a true Heaven, for we all will be the light of the world.

51

Life Needs No Purpose

So now one is Awakened, so what is the purpose of life now, what more is there to do? Well of course there is nothing that needs to be done, why does life need a purpose, isn't just being alive enough? Do the birds need a purpose to be happy? Of course not, they're busy being birds. Ask a child who is playing why does he play, he will laugh at you and think you're mad. The trouble is as we grow and become educated we are told that we have to find purpose in our lives to be happy—we need a PhD to be really happy—because of this false view we then try to become successful, a somebody, and all we do is become a miserable nobody.

The mind body is born from pure Being but we are not the mind body, we are pure Being, but why a body from pure being. Again there is no reason, its just what IS. As soon as we put a reason to everything we then feel as though we have to keep up with these reasons or purposes, everything is life being life, a rock is life also, even though its an inanimate object it still has everything that is contained in the Universe within it.

Now that there is Awareness in your life, you will realise that you no longer need to have a purpose, you now live in the moment of NOW, not in the past or a dreamt future. We still make arrangements for what still needs to be done in the so called future, with such things as family affairs or work, but we don't now make it our life purpose, as if we won't be happy until this purpose is met. If things ain't met then so be it, we just continue to the next stage of life, without taking the past or future into it.

Because we now live in the present we are no longer under the influence of the ego, which is trying its hardest to keep us in its drama of an illusionary dream. We have now Awakened from this dream and have realised the whole game that we were playing, a game where there was only one winner, the ego. Because the ego was the only winner in our dream world it also wants to be the winner in everyone else's dream world, and so we have wars and fighting.

Now by being Awake we catch out others ego's trying to bring us into their dream, because we don't go along with their game they cannot work out why. They will think that you are trying to be better than them or they may think that you no longer like them, they will try to become the victim and make you the villain, these are the games that the neurotic ego will play on you.

You see all sorts of games played by the ego in relationships, politics, and even from the media, the ego is always trying to make its story more dramatic than it really is. It wants to be noticed as much as possible, in fact it will even murder to be noticed, at least now I have my picture on the front news page and everyone knows who I am. Without its story it's nothing and this is what happens when we Awaken, we end the story, a story of nothing but lies and tragedy.

So what is this thing we call the ego, when a child is born into or should I say out of this world, the first thing he notices is not who he is but what is out there, his senses are all that there is to guide him. He feels the touch of his mother, he tastes the milk from her breast, he hears her voice and all these messages are accumulating within his self awareness. As he becomes older more and more messages are added to what he believes to be his life awareness, but all this accumulation is not who he is, this is all what he has obtained through his senses as the mind body organism, and of course we need to do this to a degree so as to navigate through our life as the mind body organism.

All that has been learnt by the child is stored in his memory and this accumulated information is called the ego, so all this accumulated information now, is who he thinks he is and all it is is just the by-product of what others have said about him, or what his senses have told him about the outside world.

The paradox is that even though the ego isn't who you truly are, it is from there that you must learn that it doesn't exist. We have to realise what is not true to realise what IS, because we are at a level where all we know is what we have been programmed to know. Even though the ego is a hindrance we also need to use it for the outside world so as to communicate with others, but in this realisation it's not really the same ego as with the illusionary ego, it's just knowing that there is stored information that can be useful and so we use it.

When we are born into a society or culture we are conditioned from that collective consciousness, of course we need to be at a certain level so as we all can live in harmony within that society or culture. But for the one who Realises his true inner SELF, he realises that he is not this collective consciousness, he Realises that he is beyond a mere collective consciousness of a society. To think this way is to be an outsider, a rebel, they want you to play the game but you're not playing, to the society this is selfishness and they are right, it is SELFishness, its being who you truly are, your SELF.

When we Awaken to our true Identity we will find that there is a chaos happening around us, we feel as if we are going against the grain of the outer world and in a sense we are, but the grain out there is an illusionary. It has no substance of its own, of course it can seem very strong because of the many mind bodies that are supporting it, but still its all an illusion.

Because we have been under the influence of the illusionary world for so long, we may even become afraid, and this is understandable. It can seem very scary when you are out on your own, in fact some will revert back to the ego for shelter, but because you have already tasted your true being you will never forget that, and in a little time you will come back out to play with your new life in freedom.

All that I have said in these writings are from my own inner Being. Of course there are words that have been used by others before me, but the point is you must, after reading or collecting information on

Awakening—no matter where you find it, from the bible or other scriptures it doesn't matter—is finally to come to your own inner Realisation, your own uniqueness.

Then instead of parroting what others have said you will become more receptive to your inner intuitional voice, as your truth arises and comes to the surface it will need words so you can convey it onto others, if that is what you would like to do with your truth. It is hard not to go out and declare this to the world, but we should let ourselves spend a little time in the Truth, let it be absorbed right through our whole Being.

52

Surviving in the World

When you feel within that you are ready to go forth and tell others about the good word or your own gospel, go out and tell others who want to listen and those who don't just leave with them a seed of truth, then when the ground of their inner spirit is ready, the seed will burst forth and grow into a beautiful new Realised Awakened Being.

I haven't said much about other ideologies or belief systems because I want you to investigate for your self, you now know the fundamentals about what there is to know about your Awakening. You realise now that you are already there and all that you need to do is to remember that you are there. Try not to place those before you, such as Buddha or Jesus up on a pedestal, for you will always be below them. When you are coming from Awareness you are where they are also, they have never been anywhere that you haven't been or are already, there is no higher place specially reserved for them.

You need not compare yourself to anyone else, no matter how Awakened they are, when you come from that inner Being within, you cannot compare it to anyone else. It arises through you in your own uniqueness, pure Consciousness its SELF has no attributes, it is what arises through your mind that now has been cleansed that any attributes are seen. Jesus had his own style compared to the Buddha, both had pure being flowing within but that pure Being was converted into who they were as the mind body organism. No mind body organism can be a totally pure Being, the mind body organism is of course pure Consciousness for there is nothing outside of what

IS, but still it is not allowing pure Consciousness in its purity to shine, just as the clouds are also part of the sun in its Oneness, but the clouds still can hide the sun.

But still when you are within your Being in that place of pure Silence, then you are One with Consciousness and within this you are Pure Being, its SELF. It's only when you come to the surface to share this experience that it becomes your own Uniqueness.

In the Realisation of Awareness one no longer needs to continue trying to be more Awakened, all you need to do is live in that Awareness and become more aware that you are now living in Awareness, this will automatically take care of its SELF, as I have said over and over there is nothing that you can do.

If you did experience a blissful feeling or in my case a feeling that I am all that there IS, you must also realise that this isn't what IS, this is still only the by-produced of Awareness. There is no need to try to recapture this experience, the experience is not what Enlightenment is, to continue to try to recapture this experience is only going to push you away from what IS.

Everything will be still the same, the only difference is that now you are Realised, and because you are Realised you now see all as it truly is, you now see all people out there as One, no cast, no culture, no country, all is One. For this reason we sometimes can be confused, we were so use to seeing all as separate, and now we still see things as separate but our inner Being sees through our inner eye, and this is how we see everything as One, it's seeing from within.

This also applies to love. Love isn't to be found outside of ourselves, we see things out there but the love that is within is always what we feel for the things outside, the outside stimulates the inner love that has always been there. It's not an emotion that is from past experience, it's not believing we need someone to complete ourselves, we are already complete in love and all we can do is share this love with others, who also have love within them that they can share— there is no need to take love from anyone, you can only share it. If we take the word love away, we can also call it our true Essence, it is what flows through everything, it flows below the surface of all materiality, we can also call it the inner Silence of all there is.

Again no matter what we call it, no matter how much we try to make it sound poetically, it is still simply our true Essence, this true Essence is what we disappear into when one Awakens, and after this disappearance we are never the same again. We could say that we have been kissed by God, and Now we are in love with all that there is, this is what is meant by God is love, we now Realise that we are love, we are all that God is.

So there is no need for you to base your life on anyone else from the past or even here and now, find your true Being and live through that true Being in your own Individual way. There is no need to throw away all that you have been conditioned, you only need to let go of that which keeps you from your true Being. You have been living your life in a prison made by your programming but now that you are free from this illusionary prison, you still keep the things that you have learnt there that has served you well. Not all in this prison life was totally worthless, so these are what we still use after the so called prison life, to serve us in or freedom from the imprisonment we put ourselves into.

So here we are now Awakened to what is really happening, we don't just magically change to a being that is no longer under the influence of the so called outer world, we just see the outer world for what it is. Now when we are lost in what we didn't realise before, we just catch these moments out and simply watch them disappear into where they came from, nowhere.

There are those who believe that once we are Enlightened we no longer are under the influence of the mind, to me this is denying what really is happening, we still need to be a human being and because we are still a human being we are going to do what human beings do. We will still feel anger, we will still feel grief and sadness, but now we are not over taken by these emotions that arise and disappear, whereas before we were drowned within them.

Enlightenment is really just our Awareness of what is happening in the world around us, it's Realising that we are all One but at the same time we need to see the so called separation, so as to find our way around the world out there. It's not some hocus-pocus mysterious thing, its just who we truly are, it only seems mysterious to the one who is searching for it, when it is remembered it then becomes the most natural thing we know, you'll wonder why you never noticed it before.

If a domesticated animal is taken back to the wild, it will either learn to survive through its natural born instincts, or it may die because its been away from its natural habitat for so long, it has forgotten how to survive. If we introduce the animal to the wild slowly letting it get used to the surroundings, and also letting it remember what food it ate when it was in its natural habitat, then the animal will have a good chance of surviving the natural life that it was meant to have.

In some ways we are the same as the domesticated animal, we have been pushed so fast into this so called advanced world that we have forgotten how to live as human beings, after all we are animals also. Could this be the reason we see so much mental illness in the so called civilised world, we are simply being pushed into something that we are not ready for.

No matter where we are in the world, be it a big city or just a small city, we can always find that place of Silence. Through the hassle of a big city there is still the silence below all the confusion, we can practice meditation if that is for you, or do as I do and just sit in a comfortable area such as a coffee shop, and just see the people moving around, and feel that stillness that is there in the background, no matter where you are it's always there. After a while you'll get used to feeling this stillness, its not that you are trying to hide and pretend that all the chaos isn't going on out there, its just that you Realise that the chaos isn't what is truly there, there is only pure Being, with whatever arising and disappearing

Within the Awakening there is a sense of great freedom, this freedom is experienced by those who have Awakened in many ways, it depends on what you were imprisoned by when you were still asleep. You may have been trying to find happiness outside of yourself and because of this you were never happy or at least totally happy. So the first thing that you may feel in the Awakening is total happiness that is so overwhelming, that you may even cry, but these tears will be tears of total joy, not sadness. You may also be one who was looking for love outside, you may have been trying to find it in many relationships, but it was never there to be found, so Awakening for you may be experienced with a deep inner love for all that is out there. You suddenly see love in all people and not just people but all things, you even now realise that you don't even need another to experience love, you are love.

We must still though keep our watch on the ego, it won't just magically disappear, it will be still there but not as powerful as it was, we are no longer feeding it as much as we did, it will slowly now die of starvation, but just like anyone who is starving it will try its hardest to eat something and that something will be you, it will again try to swallow your whole Being. This doesn't mean that we should now become paranoid with everything that we do, it just means that we need to be alert, like the detective I spoke of earlier, just catching it out and seeing for what it is, nothing.

Try not to be drawn into arguments on what you have experienced in your Awakening, if you have had a genuine Awakening why try to argue about it being more genuine than someone else's Awakening. If someone argues about your personal experience, all you need to do is just listen and realise that they could never know of your experience, and if they had their own experience, well they wouldn't be arguing in the first place.

I found myself being drawn into silly arguing over what is and what is not Enlightenment, all I was trying to do was let them know that it doesn't matter, we are all that there is right NOW. But still they wanted to argue that it wasn't that easy and that I wasn't Enlightened myself. I then tried to explain that no, I wasn't Enlightened as who I or they thought I was, that being Robert, but there was a disappearance into pure Being and that was experienced through Robert but not by Robert, and still they argued.

Just be honest with yourself and don't try to be something that you're not, don't try to be some higher than thou, for the ego will try its best to take hold of even your experience in Consciousness, it will try to own it for itself, if you allow this then you will be confused. You will then start to question your Awakening and this will put you into a situation where you start to believe that more needs to be done, all that needs to be done is to Realise that you are there, and all doubting is from the ego that is making you believe you ain't there, this will be seen for what it is, an illusion full of piss and wind.

So again just be honest with yourself, if there has been an authentic Wakening then believe me you will know, it really makes no sense for me to go on trying to tell you exactly how one should experience their own Awakening. As I have already said it all depends on the person who has Awakened, it also depends on what was the most powerful thing that kept you asleep. This will influence what you feel from within, for it must still come through the mind body and what is still there from the ego will have some influence on the experience.

It is a good idea for you to keep this to yourself for some time, silently let it become your whole being, let it absorb right through your every cell. Yes the ego residue will be still there but just remember to keep seeing for what it is, it cannot hurt you, it has no substance of its own, it only has power over you if you give your power over to it.

Also beware of those who believe they are experts in the field of spirituality, they will attack you with all their theories of why you are not Enlightened. The philosophy of what people believe to be Enlightenment is never going to prove anything, it will never understand what is or what isn't Enlightenment, they are mere words, they are second-hand. Remember also what I am sharing is also second-hand, you must find your own way to describe your Awareness, you may of course use what others have shared as your tools also, as they would have used others also before them.

53

Sharing Your Awareness

I have found that those who are Awakened don't try to tear others down, they don't try to argue over one being Enlightened and the other not, they will usually not give you anything, for what could they give you that you already haven't got? They will only give you pointers as you will yourself when fully absorbed in your own Awareness. You will know of those who are Wakened by their deep interest in your own beautiful Awareness, you will have something that both of you can share and have at least some understanding of each others experience.

Because the Realisation in Awareness is such a rare thing, you may at times feel a little lonely, that is because you haven't got someone who has also Realised their awareness, or someone else to talk about this new found inner love. You will want to share it with someone because of your deep compassion, even though this is harmless it can become a hazard if you let it overtake you, the ego will take advantage of it and turn it into a wanting. It will want to find what seems harmless into a deep clinging, a deep clinging to have someone to listen to its story, a story of how it became Awakened, it will have no interest in the genuine Awakening at all. What helped me was to read about others who also had a genuine Awakening, you will find them, you will be drawn to them because you will recognise them by the truth that they speak of.

Jesus answered and said unto him, "Verily, verily I say unto thee, unless a man be born again, he cannot see the Kingdom of God."

John 3:3

When we are finally Awakened we are as if it were, born again, the old false self is now seen for what it was, just an illusion that made us believe it was who we were. As Jesus said "unless we are born again, we cannot see the Kingdom of God". Of course this Kingdom is our pure Being, our true SELF in Consciousness. The old self being the veil that kept the most holy place deep within hidden is now dissolved, or is now in the process of dissolving, to reveal the true SELF that was hidden, this is the kingdom that was promised to us from our deeper intuitive voice of God.

You are now within your true being, the Christ that has returned, you were always the Christ but you forgot this and now your remembrance has returned to you. The clouds that hide your Divine Essence are now rolled away and there in all its beauty, is the beauty that all will one day see, the beautiful inner being of true Divine Love.

In this Kingdom of God there are the Mansions that are made for those who have Awakened, there they shall dwell and from there they shall send their message forward to all those who have ears to listen. These Mansions are the higher levels of Consciousness, when we are resting within them we draw from there the Love of God, this Love is a never ending flow of pure Essence, it will be so overflowing throughout our lives now that we are Awakened, that we cannot do anything but share from this deep Ocean well. Our lives now will never be the same again, we should at this stage at least try to learn how to share this inner Being, of course if that's what you want to do, there are no rules.

Even those who decide not to share their story of their Awakening, are still actually doing a lot for humanity, by being who they are now, pure Being, they help to lift humanity up into a higher Consciousness, for we are all One, within One body and that body is known as the Christ.

I have used the language of the bible to describe the inner Self as the Christ, but you can use any scriptures to come to the same inner meaning. This is where it is a good idea to try and read other scriptures that you may not be familiar with, when you have Awakened you will see the truth everywhere around you. You will see it in nature, you will see it in all people around you, you will see it in the starry night, you will even see in the pockets of war that are fought around the world. There is no place that truth cannot be found, for God is Omnipresent, and where God is, there you are to be found also. You are now a new creature, a new man or woman, you are the light of the world, so go out now and let your beautiful light shine, that all may one day Awaken to their own inner light, their own true Self.

54

Remember to Remember

I don't see myself as a teacher or any Guru type guy, they do have their place but its not for me, you yourself are all you need to find your true Self, your true Being. As I have said over and over you are all ready there, there is nothing outside of you that needs to be found.

All I can do really is just keep repeating over and over the same message, but you need to go beyond the message, don't get lost in my words or anyone else's words, no matter how beautiful they sound to you—they are still just words.

We have been so programmed to live by words and concepts, that we forget to listen from our inner Being that is always communing with us, that still small voice that you hear within you is not an imaginary voice. This voice within at first seemed to me as if I was going mad or psychotic, as I have said I didn't understand anything about this weird world of inner Being, and because of my mental illness or the mind body organisms mental illness it just came through me all jumbled up. I was in pure Consciousness but at this time in my apparent life I couldn't swim, I couldn't integrate with this inner calling, I was thrashing about, confused and paranoid of all that was happening.

Because of the powerful influences on the mind caused by programming and conditioning over many years, we or our inner Self is so smudged over with all the crap just like a mirror with grime on its surface, that only a little light shines through but not enough for full clarity. This is why we are so overcome by the two so called worlds colliding together, this in my case was the reason for my confusion with true Reality.

There are many names for this confusion, the dark night of the soul, being in the wilderness, are just two such names, but its all the same, its just the two worlds colliding, one an illusion and the other what IS, that which is your true inner Being, your true Self. When this confusion takes over just relax and know that you are all that there Is, just keep letting yourself know your true position in the bigger picture. From there see the insignificance of what you thought was your world, the world of illusion.

By keeping yourself in this inner Silence and reminding yourself of your position in the bigger picture, you will after some time become who you truly are. You are already that but the mind is tricking you over and over that your not. Die daily as Paul said somewhere in the scriptures, this dying daily will help you to remember each day that you are not just this little dot called a human being, this will also help you get through the so called dark night of the soul, the wilderness, and by this you will gradually become acquainted with your true inner Self, you will begin to live from there more and more each day.

In some ways it can be a burden to hear this. When we hear that we are more than who we thought we were, this sets up a mission to be accomplished, a path that we become so eager to find that we can spend our whole life trying to find it.

Many on this mission become so frustrated that they then forget to live in the Now. They waste their whole life trying to find who they already are, even after hearing this truth that they are already there is not enough, they miss the point of the message that points to their true Self, and only see the outer message, the outer husk with the kernel of truth within.

But even so we will only do what we can, if there is grace it will happen, so really it doesn't matter in the end what we do, after all everything is just perfect just how it is, it can never be any other way.

YOU ARE ALREADY THERE

There are many so called techniques out there, these can be helpful but only again if one is under the grace of their calling home, as I said this calling home is within all of us. It just happens to show on the outer world in so many ways, it can be continuing to fall in what we believe to be love, but this seems to never satisfy us and so we continue still trying to find what is within on the outer world, but there it can never be found.

All is there for the taking, it doesn't cost thousands of dollars travelling around the world, you don't need to go to India to find a Guru or teacher. Of course there is nothing wrong with this but just remember you don't need to, you are already there, you just need to remember that you are there. This remembrance won't be from the mind, it will be like looking in a mirror and seeing your Self for the first time, then there's the 'yes', I remember now, it has all come back to me.

This remembrance cannot be put into words, it must be from your own Being, this Being is all that there IS, its mine also, it belongs to all, no matter what religion or belief system you belong to, it is what is buried below the scriptures. You must dig deep to find this treasure for it has been covered over by many years of dogma and fundamentalist crap and this is what has made it stink so bad.

Just like a pure pearl that has been thrown into the mud, it seems now like a dirty piece of wet dirt, that is until we wash the mud off the pearl and reveal the beauty underneath. You are this pearl, you have been buried under all of your programming and conditioning, go below the surface of all this crap and there you are, there you are in all your beauty, this is your Self Remembrance. It's remembering your true Nature and this remembrance will automatically set you into its Oneness, its pure Love and there you will commune from forever more.

55

The World We Make

S o here I am and everyone else tossing words around such as Consciousness, Being, Enlightenment, Awakening and so it goes on and on, so lets just forget about this weird language and see it from a childlike way.

We are born or should I say the mind body organism is born from the world, we then call this organism a human being. This is no different than an animal being born from the world, lets say a dog, for we are only animals as well, we are no higher or lower, just an animal.

The only difference is that we have a larger brain that makes it possible to live our life much more different than all other animals, it doesn't mean we are better, in most cases we get ourselves into much worse situations than any animal on the face of this planet ever could.

But still here we are, this mind body organism that has been equipped with senses that make it possible to navigate the body through this so called life that we live. What we call the outside world is only there because we have made it what we believe to be our outside world, it is no more than a soup of vibrating molecules and atoms. Over millions of years of evolutionary change we have become accustomed to this soup, and because of this we have arranged all this into our psyche and therefore this is what keeps us living this life we know now.

So all we are is just an organism that is living its life just like all other organisms, so this is really all it is, everything else is what we imagine it to be. Because we have pleasure senses we have found millions of ways to satisfy this pleasure such as our over indulgence into sexual pleasures, our over indulgence into the satisfaction of food and so the list goes on.

We have also made our breeding habits an indulgence, we have dressed it up in a cloak of emotional fantasy, calling it love. We write poetry, sing songs and believe that we have heartache when the other doesn't match our own emotional wishes and programming.

Because of this—and remember this has been growing to what it is now over millions of years—to hear this as I have described above is outrageous to the now programmed mind body organism. How dare I say that we are just an organism swimming in a sea of soup, where is your heart? It will attack anyone who goes against this multi million year old story, a story that it will even kill for.

So basically that's the story of our emergence from our home in Consciousness, or life, knowing this now we can relax and just live a life that we now know is basically built on the pleasure of our senses. In other words just live life and enjoy your life, knowing also that everyone else is the same, therefore we should let all others enjoy their life, its that simple.

A child doesn't dress up what he or she experiences into something that it's not. They either like you for who you are or they don't like you, it's no big deal to them, the next time they see you they may like you for no reason. When we become adults, if we don't like someone we hold a grudge for as long as a life time in most cases, everything becomes a huge drama and we become so miserable that we project this misery onto everyone else around us making everyone else miserable.

We take this neurotic behaviour throughout our life applying it to just about everything we do, this is one reason I left the life of having a relationship, it was just too complicated and after all I wasn't after anything to make me happy. I now realised that true happiness was bubbling within me all along.

When one becomes aware of what Is, they see more and more of the drama that is all around them, they can even become someone who just wants to be alone, not lonely but just the enjoyment of being alone with all that there Is. They have realised that they lack nothing and no longer need anything to make them happy.

As I have already said earlier in the book, when I was a child everything around me was so exciting, I use to wonder off alone and explore the world around me. I never seem to lose that childlike adventure within me, I believe now that that may have been my grace that led me to the apparent Awakening, the grace of being child like, the grace of seeing beyond what most were seeing, at least as an adult.

Of course this doesn't mean we should all act like children, after all nothing would ever be done, no, what I mean is we should try to keep our childlike tendencies, our innocence, not being childish which is totally different. When we lose this inner child we become someone who is trying to find their happiness, they try to fill this inner void, and yes they can become childish for the simple reason that they just don't know how to be this inner child. They have been too long away from their true inner child, and what they are doing is trying to be something they're not. They are trying to be the actual child that they once were but they can never be who they once were, that child has died but what is within that child can never die, it's always within you.

56

From Artificial to the Real

So now we no longer need to make everything into what it isn't, we don't have to make happiness into something that we need to feel emotionally about, or to make what we call love into a violin background emotional story. Happiness is just what we are and therefore everything we do just stimulates what is already within, the same with love, we are love and whoever we decide to be with will also stimulate what is already within, it was always there, do you remember Now?

I suppose what I am trying to say is that, it's no big deal, we are all naturally what IS, it's just our mind or the way we use the mind that makes it seem so difficult. Even after hearing this there are many that just can't realise that they are already there, they want something to cling to, something to make them feel as if the journey is all worth it.

Again, you are already there, stop pretending you're not, because this is all you are doing, pretending. It's time to stop playing this game, in fact it's time to stop playing any game that is made by the ego mind. It's great to play games but only when you know its a game, otherwise you are caught in a game that you have no idea that you are playing. This is what is happening all the time around the world, we are drawn into the political game and even at times are drawn into their games of war, with real bullets and bombs that kill, this is no fun game and yet we all get sucked into it.

It's time for all to wake up and see what's there in front of us. It's time to take off the blinkers that have only shown partially what's actually there in front of our nose. It's time to grow up, not as a so called adult, gee, that has never worked, but to grow up spiritually. Grow up to our true Self, from there we will begin a whole new life that has very rarely been lived on the face of this planet.

In this new life we will not see each other as being a different race, or colour, not someone who belongs on another part of the earth and believing that their part is better than your part. This way of living is the childish way, it just doesn't belong in a world of spiritual maturity. We have been acting like spoiled dangerous children, that can bring misery on themselves and everyone else, and until this culture of childishness ceases, we will never be free as a higher Consciousness species of animal.

So all we really want from life is just to be happy and free, just like all other life forms do. It's as simple as that, all else is just added into our life to bring nothing but misery—a simple life is really the best life—why complicate things and make it into some stupid drama as most of us do, in the case of what we call love for example, just take a look at the soapies and shudder at the thought of living a life as such.

So when this Realisation that you are already there comes to your memory, that is beyond the mind, its more like an inner recognition. A recognition that all is well and always has been. Then you will begin to really live, just simply being who you are, an animal who has risen in Consciousness and can now reap the benefits of being in that state, after all it took you billions of what we call years to get there, now enjoy your life for once.

So now that we realise who we truly are what's next? Well nothing really, we just simply live our life naturally just the way it is meant to be lived. The ego will want to find another excuse to keep itself on the path, a path that will never let you live a truly peaceful life.

The ego can never be satisfied, there are many who spend their whole lives trying to achieve their dreams—it could be to have more money, a perfect relationship, a work position or whatever—but when they finally get to where they want to be, they seem to be still unhappy. This is because it was never their inner calling that was satisfied, this inner calling was confused with what they felt to be on the outer side, and because it was on the outer side it could never be true happiness of realising that you are all ready there. You must also realise that once we Realise that we are there, that is to truly Realise with all your inner Being, then to want to achieve anything else is just that. To achieve something else, you are no longer trying to achieve anything because you need to, you are only trying to achieve it because you can, and if you don't achieve it, then that's ok as well.

Now to understand all this intellectually, that is with the mind, is not enough, we must have an understanding from deep within, this understanding is felt intuitively, it's an understanding where there is no doubt. You now know intuitively, deep within, that it is truth, but not a truth that becomes a concept or turned into a belief that you then must adhere to, no, this is how the scriptures have come about and then made into a dogma, which then becomes a fundamentally followed belief system or religion.

This is as far as I can lead you, from here you must discover deep within this inner truth for yourself, and like I have said, when this inner truth is discovered there will be no doubt. You will in fact stop asking so many questions, if you do keep asking questions, all your going to get is second-hand knowledge, no matter where this knowledge comes from or even who it comes from, it will always be second-hand.

Everything in this book or any book is always second-hand, after the words have soaked into your inner being and there has been an inner stimulation, an igniting of your inner Being, then and only then will you really Know, then and only then will you be satisfied and complete.

Again, don't ever put anyone or anything that you believe to be the truth up on a pedestal, this has already been the case with so many religions, they put their favourite God man up high that they can never reach them. They continue to quote everything they say, they continue to read the scriptures over and over that they know them by heart, but this will never shift you from your prison that they have kept you in. It's time to break free from these prisons and discover the wonders that are within you, waiting for you to discover.

Most believe that once they have obtained this inner Awareness that from then on they are going to be living a life of Blissfulness, that they will never be sad again, they believe that their life from now on will be a bed of roses. Because of this expectation they then become disappointed when they realise that it's just not going to be like that.

When one has come to Realise the truth, their life continues on just the way it always has, but the difference is that their life now is no longer under the illusion that they are separate from all else. They see that all that is happening is just what is arising from Consciousness, neither good or bad, they no longer judge what they used to as being something bad happening to them, or even something good happening to them, it's just there, happening.

In this way in living through the truth we no longer see the tragic happenings throughout the world as something evil, or as if some God is not happy with us and wants to bestow his wrath upon us for being naughty children. We realise that all that is happening is just what is happening, no one or anything to be blamed for. To live any other way is to live in fear of what you believe to be out there, when in fact there is nothing out there, out there is also within, all is One—it only seems to be that way because of your mind body organisms programming.

When you finally Realise this, the fear that you once had will begin to slowly disappear. It took many years to build this illusion that you have of being separate, and because of this you cannot expect change in your perception overnight, after all there's still the mind body that is lived through.

The inner Being is the innocence that I earlier called your inner childlikeness, it's your true Self and it knows nothing of what the outer mind believes itself to be. It's like the waves on the ocean, no matter how rough or calm the waves are it matters not to the stillness below the waves, deep beneath the ocean is the vastness of all that the waves are formed from. This is no different from what we call our outer world, all the ups and downs of our life that we label good or bad are no different than the waves upon the ocean, below all this perception is the stillness that you truly are.

What we call Enlightenment or Awakening, is when we as the waves upon the ocean disappear back into the ocean, we now realise that we are the ocean and we always have been the ocean. We now can surface and play upon the ocean of Consciousness, just as we play with the waves when surfing or swimming. Even when the waves become rough and are tossing us about, we will still realise that below all this is the calm and silent peacefulness, that we all truly are.

So what if we are happy with our life just the way it is, what if we have no need to be Realised or Awakened, well to that I would say fantastic! That's just how it should be, after all the only reason I was accidentally Awakened was that I was totally lost in the confusion of what I couldn't understand, I just gave into life and life gave to me.

Therefore if one is happy—and I mean truly happy—with their life then why would one want to be so called Enlightened or Awakened? After all when one is truly Awakened all they can do is to come back to the life that they are living and simply enjoy it. I have noticed that many traditional families, an example being the Italians, seem to be very happy people, they love their family life, they love their food and they seem to love life generally. I also notice that there isn't a big call for Enlightenment in these communities and the reason I believe is that why would they want it, they're doing exactly what we should as a living being, just being happy, no more, no less.

There is no need to become Enlightened and then walk around thinking "hey!, I'm Enlightened." As I keep saying you're already there, you have always been there. The ones who are naturally always happy and are not looking for anything to make them happy, are in a way living an Enlightened life, without knowing that they are living an Enlightened life, these are the fortunate ones, the one who we all can learn from.

But unfortunately these communities are becoming more scarce as we become more so called advanced. We are wanting everything out there, the new cellular phones, the new digital televisions, iPods and on and on it goes, we are not happy until we get all these carrots that are dangled in front of us. Because of this we are forgetting about the simple things in life, we don't notice the flower that popped up out of nowhere as we walk to the front gate, we forget that there is a shower of beautiful stars just above us each night, we are totally blind to all that is around us.

Because of this our life is becoming even more artificial, we as the mind body organism are already artificial compared to the real deal, and here we are making it even more artificial. We have made artificial love, artificial happiness, and even artificial enlightenment, yes we are after instant enlightenment, just like instant coffee, add and stir, or pay to go to a retreat and there you have it, instant enlightenment.

Of course going to a retreat has its benefits but it will never make you Enlightened, if you are under the grace of who you already are, then there may be a remembrance that only needed that little push for you to remember, "oh yes that's it, its all coming back to me." But this can happen only if you are already there, as you already are, the retreat, the book, the speaker, the scriptures were like the straw that broke the camel's back. It was already going to happen and it just needed that little push, that piece of straw. In my case it was just giving into what Is, and what Is gave to me all that Is. Its your turn now to experience for yourself, the treasure that is found deep within you, its been there all along, the key to your true Being is truly you, and after all, you are already there.

Thoughts of Freedom

The iron shackles cast off by desire.
Become the golden chains
That bind one tighter.
Freedom is desireless.
To free oneself from the pursuit of security and power,
One mentally creates its opposite. But in doing this, one
Is merrily creating another set of securities, only calling
Them by another form of security even though it is called
Love, humility, service, following truth.
Awareness of the false, as false, is freedom of truth.

Palden

Thoughts of Grace

I act So,
I am Spontaneously
I am, Grace.

Perceive the barriers that surround you, and when you
Have discerned them, you will be rid of them yourself,
And not reshaping yourself to fit some other pattern.
When you yourself break through these patterns and
Systems, your action becomes spontaneous.
When You free the mind and heart from the many barriers
That shut them in, then there is the flow of reality.

Spontaneous action is Grace

Palden

I Am That

I am That
Believe not a word
I say But take yourself to that place
That place between the words
I speak
That place between the notes
I play
That place between the vision
I see
That place of no place
I am
That is Love

I am That.

The word spoken, the note played, the vision seen
Lost in the moment, a will-ó-'wisp
Look not for the new word, the new note, the new vision
Dwell in that place, before it has arisen

I am That.

The voice, the ears, the eye's of the creative energy
are within;
Within the place
Within the silence
Within

I am That.
The word, the note, the vision
Tainted by its memory
Live only in the mind.
I live
The pure truth
Between
Awaiting in silence
To come forth, again
As love.
I am That

Palden

The Myth of Love

The great myth of love is that you can love someone,
Something or yourself. No one can love another! You
Cannot love yourself or anyone else. Why? Because love
Is not doing, but allowing. The very energy from which
This universe is built is infused with a certain quality-a
Joy of being, an acceptance of the right of all things to be
And a delight in the expressions of all things, as they enjoy
Their right to be. All beings are the Source and have a divine
Right to experience and express their divinity, and all beings
Have a right to enjoy the expression of others, because all Beings
Are really One, cleverly disguised to look separate.

Palden